REMBRANDT'S MIRROR

Part Three of

EUROPA

a tetralogy

Poetry

Collected Poems 1960–1984
Nightingales: Poems 1985–1996

Plays

Agora — a Dramatic Epic,
in chronological order of action
consisting of:

Healing Nature — The Athens of Pericles
Virgil and Caesar ⎤
Moving Reflections ⎬ Roman Trilogy
Light Shadows ⎦
Byzantium
Living Creation — Medici Florence ⎤
King Francis I
Rembrandt's Mirror ⎬ Europa Tetralogy:
Goethe's Weimar ⎦
A Conception of Love
Maquettes for the Requiem Trilogy of One Act plays
Lying Figures ⎤
Killing Time ⎬ Requiem Trilogy
Meeting Ends ⎦

Editor

Eleven Poems by Edmund Blunden
Garland
Studies in the Arts

REMBRANDT'S MIRROR

a play by Francis Warner

Men klaagt, indien de balsem stort,
Om 't spillen van den dieren reuk;
Maar niet, zo 't glás bekoomt een breuk,
Als 't edel nat geborgen wordt.

Vondel: *Elegy for Dionys*

OXFORD THEATRE TEXTS 14
COLIN SMYTHE, GERRARDS CROSS, 2000

First published in 2000 by Colin Smythe Limited
Gerrards Cross, Buckinghamshire

Warner, Francis. 1937–
Rembrandt's Mirror: a play — (Oxford Theatre Texts,
ISSN 0141–1152; 14)

ISBN 0–86140–432–7

Distributed in the United States of America by
Dufour Editions, PO Box 7, Chester Springs, PA 19425

The publishers and author acknowledge with gratitude
permission given by the named galleries to reproduce
the colour slides as indicated in the text

Cover design and production photographs by
Billett Potter of Oxford

Produced in Great Britain
Printed and Bound by
T. J. International Ltd., Padstow, Cornwall

FOR NICOLAAS RUPKE

REMBRANDT'S MIRROR was produced by the Oxford University Dramatic Society (OUDS) for performance in the Garden Quadrangle Auditorium, St. John's College, Oxford on Tuesday, May 11th, 1999.
The director was Tim Prentki.

The cast was as follows:

Maurits	*Oliver Williams*
Frederik Hendrik	*Mark Payton*
William II	*Oliver Williams*
Constantijn Huygens	*Ben Lester*
Joost van den Vondel	*Daniel Cassiel*
Pieter Lastman	*Simon Breden*
Rembrandt van Rijn	*Simon Kane*
Titus van Rijn	*Benedict Warner*
Jan Lievens	*Adrian Gillott*
Carel Fabritius	*William Turner*
Samuel van Hoogstraeten	*Tom Bowtell*
Johannes Vermeer	*Mark Evans*
Rev. Adriaen Smout	*Darren Ormandy*
Rev. Jacobus Trigland	*Ian Drysdale*
Thomas Haringh	*Ian Drysdale*
Saskia van Uylenburgh	*Nicole Evans*
Geertge Dircx	*Rachel Fishwick*
Hendrickje Stoffels	*Claire Griffin*
Maria Visscher	*Mary Ann Lund*
Cornelia van Rijn	*Miranda Warner*
Isiciata	*Laura Knightly-Brown*
Sappho	*Charlotte Hunt-Grubbe*
Lesbia	*Sarah McKendrick*

Lighting David Colmer with Kyle Collins. Slides Amy Faerber. Help in obtaining slides Dr Christopher Brown, Director, Ashmolean Museum. Slide projection and sound system Lighting and Sound Equipment, Oxford. Sound Karl Shikles. Costumes Penelope Warner with the Royal Shakespeare Company and Birmingham Costume Hire. Hair styles Elaine Kershaw. Speelhouse advisor Lotte C. Van de Pol. Dutch pronunciation Kristin Ladenburg. Script and computer Leslie Hager. Stewards Jane Burnett, Karen Cheung, Angie Gilbert, Leslie Horton, Jackie Park, Emily Parker, Lesa Pastor, Andrea Porrello, Michael Van Cise, Margaret Wendell, Paul William, Taha Yarahmad. Props Brad Bowlby, Amy Davidson, Brandon Faircloth, Julie Merritt. Stage Manager Jennifer Graebner. OUDS President Matt King.

Characters

Maurits	*Prince of Orange*
Frederik Hendrik	*Prince of Orange, younger half-brother of Maurits*
William II	*Prince of Orange, son of Frederik Hendrik*
Constantijn Huygens	*Secretary to Frederik Hendrik*
Joost van den Vondel	*Poet*
Pieter Lastman	*Artist, tutor of Lievens and Rembrandt*
Rembrandt van Rijn	*Artist*
Titus van Rijn	*Rembrandt's son*
Jan Lievens	*Artist*
Carel Fabritius	*Artist, Rembrandt's pupil*
Samuel van Hoogstraeten	*Artist, Rembrandt's pupil*
Johannes Vermeer	*Artist*
Rev. Adriaen Smout	*Preacher of the Reformed Church*
Rev. Jacobus Trigland	*Preacher of the Reformed Church*
Thomas Haringh	*Bailiff of Insolvency Court, Auctioneer*
Saskia van Uylenburgh	*Rembrandt's wife, mother of Titus*
Geertge Dircx	*Rembrandt's mistress*
Hendrickje Stoffels	*Rembrandt's mistress, mother of Cornelia*
Maria Visscher	*Poet*
Cornelia van Rijn	*Rembrandt's daughter*
Isiciata	*(first letter pronounced eye-) Procuress*
Sappho	*Woman of Pleasure*
Lesbia	*Woman of Pleasure*

The play is set in Holland between the years 1625 and 1672 A.D.

There are two acts.

Act One

PIETER LASTMAN *'s studio, on the Breestraat,*
Amsterdam, 1625.

LIEVENS   Charcoal!

REMBRANDT   Pardon?

LIEVENS   Charcoal's the nickname
I'll give you now we've come to Amsterdam.

REMBRANDT   Jan Lievens; then I'll call your glow 'Burnt out' –
Although at eighteen you should have some
          future ...

LIEVENS   Just because you're nineteen! Look! I came
          here
To study under Pieter Lastman's brush
Aged ten – that was my easel for two years!

REMBRANDT   Poor Lastman, putting up with you! I want
To meet this master painter. What did you
          learn?

LIEVENS   How to prepare a canvas, and grind colours,
Pounce powdered charcoal over pulp ...

REMBRANDT   Why
          'charcoal'?
Why call me that?

LIEVENS   You've been to Latin school.
'Rem' 'brandt', thing burnt, coal charred ...

REMBRANDT   What's
          Lastman like?

LIEVENS   Rueful that we've retreated from the plague
                 In Leiden to plague him. I'll introduce you.
                 He's seen a little of your work – not much;
                 But frowns that gloomy Swanenburgh has
                           taught you.

REMBRANDT   While you were studying with Lastman, here.

LIEVENS   How different! Lastman's clear Italian light,
                 And occult Swanenburgh's dark underworld
                 Of Virgil's Sibyl – why, his 'Witches' Sabbath'
                 Flung Swanenburgh before the Inquisition!

REMBRANDT   His court-connections saved him.

LIEVENS   Was he tutor
                 To our own polymathic diplomat
                 Constantijn Huygens?

REMBRANDT   No. His cousin was.

LIEVENS   Constantijn Huygens! I must paint his pose –
                 Hands clasped, lips pursed, eyes middle-
                           distanced: Huygens
                 Burns in my visual dreams.

REMBRANDT   You *mean* he can
                 Commission pictures from us for the Prince
                 Maurits – and the Council of the State
                 Bows to his taste and judgement. Maurits' half-
                           brother,
                 The playboy Frederik Hendrik loves all art:
                 Palaces, music, ladies ...

                 Enter LASTMAN.

LASTMAN   Hullo, Lievens!
                 So this is Rembrandt of the Rhine you've
                           brought
                 To show me?

LIEVENS   Yes, sir.

LASTMAN   Glad to see you both.
            (To REMBRANDT*)* What is your greatest fear?

REMBRANDT   Oh,
                  to go blind.

LASTMAN   Good answer! Are you Catholic? I am.
             Well, you don't have to answer; but this town
             Is being wrecked by Calvin. On one side
             Those who remonstrate against his harshness,
             Then, on the other, the Counter-Remonstrants.
             Just keep your head down if you work for me:
             Leopards select the strutting chimpanzee.

REMBRANDT   Did you look at my work?

LASTMAN   Yes; but not now.
             We'll discuss later. What you need 's a much
             More varied palette. Try a lower viewpoint.
             Learn to group figures, the language of
                   gesture.
             Have you a canvas there?

REMBRANDT   Yes. That one's mine.

LASTMAN   Bring it along; and Lievens, you've one, too?

LIEVENS   This boy, blowing on hot coal ...

LASTMAN   Why, that's good!
             I've two engravings of Gerard van Honthorst's:
             One on your theme, this other he's just sent –
             A lush 'Procuress'. Here's what we shall do.
             Rembrandt and Lievens, in your home town,
                   Leiden,
             It may be different, but in Amsterdam
             The brothel is the daily meeting-place
             Of artists, government inspectors, drapers,

Musicians, and all arts that stop for lunch.
My father's job – as Orphans' Beadle – was
To run the city's brothels decently
(Only the Sheriff's men, and Civil Servants,
Were trusted with such licences) so we
Lived by the Pijlsteeg – small street off the Dam
Reserved for brothels: 'speelhouses' we call
     them –
And mother sold the whores second-hand
     clothes.
Father would do embroidery to help her.
He lost his job; but through this work they
     found
A painter, choosing girls to pose for him,
Who took me on: Gerrit. His brother was
Town-organist, Jan Sweelinck, the composer
Who first invented fugue. Gerrit loves groups –
Painting historical scenes, and crowded
     triptychs.
He'd studied art in Rome, and so sent me.
Our speelhouse is next door – just one of three
Popular in this street. We all meet there
For business and for leisure. The whores sew,
Spin, knit, and serve – they make good
     pancakes! All
Dress lavishly. It's lunchtime. Lift those frames,
And join the Breestraat's intellectual games!

Exeunt.

SCENE TWO

The Speelhouse. SAPPHO *and* LESBIA.
*Music : Handel, 'Ottone', Act II: duet, Gismonda
and Matilda 'Notte cara, a te si deve'.*

SAPPHO   I love your new dress, Lesbia!

LESBIA   Do you like it?

Oh Sappho, am I beautiful?

SAPPHO
                                        You are
My love, you are! Turn round and show – walk
      proud!
None of the tulips that make men so mad
These days is daring to compete with you.

LESBIA
Most of my money goes on food, so this –
Paid for by Madam – will have to be earned
Like tulips from extended time in beds!

SAPPHO
One tulip – yes, I think it was a 'Viceroy' –
Was sold last week to an infatuated
Polder farmer for – would you believe it? –
A dozen sheep, one thousand-weight of cheese,
Eight pigs, four oxen, two ox-heads of wine,
Four tons of butter, clothes, a silver beaker,
And, thrown in last to win the bid, a bed!

LESBIA
This for a single tulip?

SAPPHO
                                    Lunacy!
One 'Semper Augustus' of one-ninety aces
Sold for two dappled horses and their coach.

LESBIA
Why, men are rocked as children in their cribs,
And then, when older, knocked between the
      ribs
By infant passions that they can't control.
I sometimes feel it's with a mother's care
I welcome home between my warming thighs
Some lost and frightened stranger, ill at ease,
When what he needs is loving arms, not knees.

Enter ISICIATA.

ISICIATA
Girls! Flouncing your court-dresses in the
      mirror?
We are the mirror to all Amsterdam

       In which it finds all that it longs to see.
       Here's work and happiness – the Prince is
           coming!

SAPPHO   Prince Frederik Hendrik? Ah! My favourite
           client.

LESBIA   He's mine, you bitch!

ISICIATA   Now don't you two girls
       quarrel!
       His secretary, Constantijn Huygens, waits.

LESBIA   That charming show-off, Constantijn.

SAPPHO   A true
       Gentleman. Who else can stroke the lute
       Till the waves pause, and all the whispering
           stars
       Hush with delight, bees hold their hum, forget
       To honey-bridge their combs? Winds hold
           their breath?
       We'll sit them down to Dutch-shipped
           Bordeaux wines,
       Sweet Malaga from Spain, South Italy's
       Sun-ripened darkness trapped in Sicily's
       Thick-tongued Marsala; not our candy syrup
       I have to toss into the potted plant
       When no one's looking.

LESBIA   That's why it wilts!

ISICIATA   I think
       Prince Maurits will rein back his wild young
           brother,
       This laughing bachelor of forty-one,
       And force him marry.

LESBIA   Sober up? What a loss!
       Prince Maurits ought to marry his own mistress

Miss frumpy Margaretha of Mechelen
And make their children legal.

ISICIATA   Disinherit
Our own heir-apparent, Frederik Hendrik,
Who cuddles us when he's home from the wars?
I'd rather swim a month in salted porridge
Than see that *freule* Margaret's children sneer.

Enter HUYGENS, FREDERIK HENDRIK *and* VONDEL.

HUYGENS   May we acquire your hospitality
For celebration of a victory?

ISICIATA   Prince Frederik Hendrik!

Women curtsey.

FREDERIK   Thank you, girls! What style! It's a far cry
From muddy siege and bloody capture of
's–Hertogenbosch. My soldiers need reward
Which only girls can give. Squeeze blood-red
wine!

VONDEL   You and your troops come home as national
heroes.
Your older brother's chain of victories
Closing the fence of frontiers south and east
Round our golden republic proved a skill
Unmatched till now: by you.

Enter LASTMAN, REMBRANDT *and* LIEVENS.

LASTMAN   May we come in?
My Prince!

FREDERIK   The artists, chefs of dreams; why,
look!
Lastman and his pupils! What have you
brought?

LASTMAN   Jan Lievens has a panel of a boy,
               Holding a pipe, blowing to redden coals.
               (Show slide no. 1, of Jan Lievens: 'Boy blowing a Pot
               of Embers' (ca. 1625) Warsaw, National Museum)

FREDERIK   Wonderful! You leave his face in shadow,
               Leading us to expect it glow with heat.

HUYGENS   Based on Antiphilus, as told by Pliny;
               Antiphilus, the rival to Apelles.

VONDEL   A learned boy!

LIEVENS   Oh no, he's just ...

REMBRANDT   Ass! You!

LASTMAN   Here is Gerard van Honthorst's version. See?
               (Show slide no. 2, of Gerard van Honthorst: 'A
               Soldier and a Girl' (ca. 1622) Braunschweig,
               Herzog Anton Ulrich-Museum)
               A soldier home on leave, warming his hand
               Lit in surrounding darkness, while half-dressed
               She blows the coal of youth's quickening
                        warmth
               Quite unresisting.

VONDEL   Perhaps Isaiah's coal
               Lifted by the rapt seraph with such tongs
               From off the altar to kiss his dumb lips
               To poetry.

HUYGENS   The dangerous fires of lust.

LESBIA   Oh, come!

FREDERIK   But look, my Constantijn, how clean
               They are, well-dressed ...

HUYGENS   Exposed.

FREDERIK Attractive! Touch,
Cup creamy beauty's thickness in her paint!
Rembrandt, what do you say? What have you
    there?

REMBRANDT He's brought the figures very near to us,
So close we'd burn from sparks between her
    tongs.
It's elegant. His other hand is strange ...

SAPPHO My honoured Prince, will you do that to me?

ISICIATA Sappho!

LESBIA And me!

ISICIATA Girls!

FREDERIK Wait! All in good time.
It's wine that squirms the oyster as we dine.
Rembrandt, show us your panel. What's it
    called?
(Show slide no. 3, of Rembrandt: 'The Music Lesson'
(1626) Bredius 632. Amsterdam, Rijksmuseum)

REMBRANDT 'The Music Lesson'.

LESBIA Why, she has my dress!

SAPPHO And my tiara!

REMBRANDT Just coincidence.

VONDEL I like the modesty that wisps her breasts.

HUYGENS 'Lot and his daughters leaving Sodom' too
On the back wall!

FREDERIK Well, the girls call the tune.
Whatever song she sings the men will play ...

LIEVENS   While the Procuress hums and waits for pay.

FREDERIK   You've used your family as models? Well,
                 Rembrandt, I want two canvasses from you
                 To give to the ambassador from England –
                 Say, a self-portrait to promote your face
                 In that wet island; and ... well, you tell me.

REMBRANDT   A portrait of my mother?

LIEVENS   Like that crone?

FREDERIK   Yes! Perfect. No one could be shocked by that.
                 You will be paid *(Gestures to* HUYGENS*)*. Lastman!
                     Delight us more!

LASTMAN   Another sent by Honthorst: a 'Procuress'
                 *(Show slide no. 4, of Gerard van Honthorst: 'The
                 Procuress' (1625) Utrecht, Centraal Museum)*

FREDERIK   The woman on the left? Our eyes look
                     breastward.

LASTMAN   And one from Dirck Baburen, who's just died,
                 With the same title.
                 *(Show slide no. 5, of Dirck van Baburen: 'The
                 Procuress' (1622) Boston, Museum of Fine Arts)*

FREDERIK   This time we can see her!

LESBIA   Isiciata, you are popular!

ISICIATA   I'm half her age! Why do they paint me ugly?

SAPPHO   To make us look more beautiful, of course.
                 Buy us a copy to hang on our wall!

FREDERIK   I shall! The man's coin will remind your guests
                 That Isiciata's finger's on her palm.
                 As for Honthorst's skill, why, if I marry

He'll be the man to paint us. *(Talks to*
                          REMBRANDT*)*

LIEVENS   Sir Constantijn, I find my sleep, thoughts, day-
         dreams
     And even meals are haunted by your face.
     (Starts sketching HUYGENS' *hands)*
     Please may I paint your clothes and ungloved
         hands
     Until you find the time to sit for me?

HUYGENS   Later. Now pay attention to the Prince.

FREDERIK   *(To* REMBRANDT*)* So you enjoy erotic poetry.
     Read up a tale of Ovid's, and then paint
     The heady image conjured in your thoughts.

HUYGENS   Diana bathing, or Callisto's shame.

REMBRANDT   I'll need a model. Which of you will pose
     To fan Prince Frederik's secret hours' repose,
     Your youth and beauty for all time disclosed?

FREDERIK   Why, both these beauties, and their friends!
         Lastman,
     Lievens come with us. Floods, plague,
         battlefields
     Fade into smoke as wine to women yields.

     Music : Handel, 'Ottone', Act II: duet, Gismonda
     and Matilda 'Notte cara, a te si deve'.
     Exeunt FREDERIK HENDRIK, HUYGENS, LASTMAN,
     LIEVENS. ISICIATA, SAPPHO *and* LESBIA *withdraw.*
     Fade scene.

SCENE THREE

VONDEL *and* REMBRANDT.

VONDEL   Young Orpheus, your 'Music Lesson' stirred

The Prince's purse to life: with two
    commissions!
That was a triumph of sheer quality.

REMBRANDT   Vondel, wait till I've painted them, then see.

VONDEL   You've squelched out of the mud and plague of
    Leiden?

REMBRANDT   To work with this great painter.

VONDEL   What's your father?

REMBRANDT   A miller.

VONDEL   And your mother?

REMBRANDT   Baker's daughter.

VONDEL   A soundly economic Dutch match.

REMBRANDT   *(Stung)* They
Were twenty-one, and in love! Look, I'm ninth
Of their ten children!

VONDEL   Are they Catholic?

REMBRANDT   Their families were, but my father, now,
Is Dutch Reformed Church, Calvinist.

VONDEL   Which sort?
Is he a modernist, a tolerant
Arminian like Oldenbarnevelt –
Lord Advocate of Holland – was: that martyr!
Or is he strictly orthodox, Gomarist,
As is Prince Maurits who beheaded his
Own friend, our Oldenbarnevelt, for spite?
This poisoned schism in our church –
    Arminian-
Remonstrant, Gomarist-Counter-Remonstrant –

Political theology, was not
There when I was a schoolboy on the Pijlsteeg,
Under old Bartjens with his cipher-book,
Where Pieter Lastman's father was the Beadle
Bringing the orphans to their desks before
Ringing the bell, opening the morning
     brothels,
Greeting my father as he passed our shop ...

REMBRANDT   Your shop?

VONDEL   Two clasped hands on the swinging
     board
Outside our silk-shop. Father passed on to me
Oh, a connoisseur's love of the fabric's
Texture, showed me you must stroke it, gently,
Helping, and teaching ladies with long nails
How, without snagging, to roll silkworm-spun
Stockings up to the thigh, then how to wash
     them ...

REMBRANDT   Your vision sounds like something out of Ovid!

VONDEL   Ah, Ovid! You were weaned on Virgil's tongue.
My parents sent me to the French school, where
We learned no Latin (though I'm learning
     now);
Just French. My family all come from Antwerp.
The Inquisition condemned Grandmother:
Pregnant, reprieved her; but my namesake,
     Joos
Vondel, the hatter, they burned at the stake
For being (like me) a Baptist. I loathe bigots!
We fled to tolerance in Amsterdam
From Spanish armies of the Duke of Alva.
My accent's still immigrant Brabant frog's-
     croak.

REMBRANDT   You like Prince Frederik Hendrik; why do you
     hate

His elder half-brother, Prince Maurits?

VONDEL   I
Loathe more the men who excommunicate
Jacob, the Admiralty brother of
My friend from the East India Company,
The poet-friendly merchant Laurens Reael.
He who denies Christians the cup of Christ
Which Jesus gave for all who'd come to him
Is an abusing tyrant!

REMBRANDT   They've damned Reael?

VONDEL   For being a gentle moderate. When two
University professors hate
Each other, all the country suffers – see,
Gomarus and Arminius, both at Leiden,
Fighting, bring plague and floods, as well as
          schism.

REMBRANDT   But who are those who expel Jacob Reael –
And his fellow Arminians? – from the church?

VONDEL   Smout and Trigland.

REMBRANDT   Pardon?

VONDEL   Trigland and
          Smout.
The Reverends Smout and Trigland:
          hypocrites.
Jacobus Trigland studied at Louvain
And only then reneged his Catholic office
To be a Calvinist. Now he hates Rome
As guilty icon of his misspent youth;
And, equally, detests all Moderates
As they imply he's got it wrong again.

REMBRANDT   I've seen the Reverend Trigland's bushy face
In Willam Delff's engraving: the long beard,

Hand on The Book, eyes staring straight at me.
But Smout?

VONDEL   Yes; well-named, smout: Old Dutch
for lard,
Melted pig's fat. I've written a new play
At the suggestion of a magistrate.

REMBRANDT   I love watching new plays. What is it called?

VONDEL   'Palamedes'. Albert Burgh, on City Council,
(Put there by Maurits of all people!) said
'Write one about the death of Barnevelt.'
'The time is not yet ripe.' I said. 'Then try
Greek allegory, like Dr. Samuel Coster's
"Iphigenia".' So I did. In mine
Agamemnon is our cruel Maurits –
Both of those sailed their fleets away to force
Their beached and stranded soldiers on the
        Trojan
Shore, or Flanders' Nieuwpoort, in despair,
Deserted, to fight better, and so win
A glorious victory – ours over the Spaniards.
Palamedes is Oldenbarnevelt:
Each suffered a rigged trial. One was stoned
To death by the Greek army; Barnevelt,
Aged seventy-two, beheaded on the cobbled
Courtyard of Prince Maurits' Binnenhof,
Outside his gothic hall, at noon.

REMBRANDT   Lunchtime!
Pieter Lastman painted 'Coriolanus
Yielding peace to his Mother' to persuade
Holland make peace with Spain. In the same
        way
I'll paint your scene: 'Palamedes Condemned';
And match it with a 'Stoning of St. Stephen'.

VONDEL   Good! To inspire you, read this that I wrote
Beside his severed body in its tomb

At dusk in the old, empty, echoing church.

VONDEL *hands* REMBRANDT *a copy of his poem. They read it aloud.*

REMBRANDT   'At the Grave of Johan van Oldenbarnevelt'

VONDEL   I am a stranger, asking – but who hears?

REMBRANDT   *Echo:* Ears.

VONDEL   Who stopped this advocate's mouth with a
          stone?

REMBRANDT   *Echo:* A throne.

VONDEL   Maurits? What broke that Prince's gratitude?

REMBRANDT   *Echo:* Altitude.

VONDEL   Did this man's free climb put freedom in
          danger?

REMBRANDT   *Echo:* Stranger!

VONDEL   Was he beheaded because he betrayed?

REMBRANDT   *Echo:* Obeyed!

VONDEL   What have the Dutch lost, cutting his poor
          thread?

REMBRANDT   *Echo:* Law dead.

VONDEL   They fought Spain to be free, yet do this act!

REMBRANDT   *Echo:* A pact.

VONDEL   What have the people learned from his sad
          fate?

REMBRANDT   *Echo:* Hate.

VONDEL   So will those sworn to Maurits live in fear?

REMBRANDT   *Echo:* Keep clear!

VONDEL   Ah! Would their pride were scythed down as
                    the grass!

REMBRANDT   *Echo:* They pass.

VONDEL   What can we do for Freedom's martyr? Gaze?

REMBRANDT   *Echo:* Praise.

VONDEL   Will the Prince, curbing Justice, trust to lashes?

REMBRANDT   *Echo:* Dust to ashes.

          Fade.

SCENE FOUR

HUYGENS, FREDERIK HENDRIK *and* PRINCE MAURITS.

HUYGENS   Your older brother wants to see you.

FREDERIK   Why?
                    I can guess. How is he?

HUYGENS   Draining away
                    With lethargy. He's an exhausted man.
                    At fifty-eight we need not call him 'old':
                    He must recover.

FREDERIK   Long years in the field
                    Of battle, with his favourite method: siege,
                    And his high office as the Stadholder
                    Of all this country's problems break his health.

HUYGENS   What worries me is that he's lost the touch
               Of victory. His popularity
               As he prevaricates, droops, and withdraws
               In listlessness, grows dangerously cold.
               With each slurred consonant he drops a
                    friend.
               Why is he dour?

FREDERIK   High office came to him
               When he was sixteen, and – what irony! –
               At Oldenbarnevelt's insistent urging
               To the Council of State. Through forty years
               Of springless winter in the public eye
               He's guided us. My father was adored,
               But far too busy to play with his son.
               His mother lived in bold adultery
               With Rubens in Cologne – the painter's father –
               Humiliating our William of Orange;
               And, as for friends, at university
               He was too young to make them. Fighting men
               Are those he feels at home with.

HUYGENS   He loves you
               More than his mistress and his children.

FREDERIK   Yes;
               Because, though I was in my mother's breasts
               Crying with newness when he was elected,
               He knows that when he dies the House of
                    Orange –
               If it survives – must be upheld by me.

HUYGENS   He calls. I'll leave you. May your warmth of
                    heart
               Glow up his embers.

MAURITS   Brother! Where are you?

HUYGENS   Make sure he drinks the liquid gold that
                    Joseph

Bueno his wise doctor has distilled.

FREDERIK   Maurits! I'm with you.

MAURITS   Yes, I'm glad you've come.
Snail-like, with scorched horns, I shrink in my
        shell,
Mosquitoes on the eyeball of my soul
Madden me into dullness as my strength
Once circling the Dutch globe narrows its proud
Ocean of expectations to a trail
Between the lavatory and my bed.

FREDERIK   But now that Oldenbarnevelt has gone
You hold all threads of power in your hands.

MAURITS   I won. The cost? To lose the will to win.
And yet, in duty, what else could I do?
For many years he had supported me,
Cared for me in my adolescence; yet
Mine is, and must be, military command
Of the whole country. He said private armies
Must swear allegiance to whatever province
Pays them; where this clashes with the State
The local, not the country, must come first.

FREDERIK   That narrow vision would destroy all peace,
Wave in our enemies, pit provinces
Against each other, fanning civil war!

MAURITS   The provinces are sovereign, in their way,
But the whole country must be sovereign, too.
Anyway, not one has a standing army.
So, without bloodshed, I sent in the troops
And, in a pageant's show of national muscle,
Disbanded their few mercenaries in
The public square at Utrecht – ordered seven
Gomarists sit in on all decisions ...

FREDERIK   And saved our country from a Catharine wheel's

Disintegration, and from Spanish teeth.

MAURITS   The country has been saved: I've killed a friend;
And that destroys the zest in any joy,
Aborts the happiness conception gives.
This is the secret every ruler hides,
Even from himself: external action then
Masks hollowness within the praising drum,
And empty trumpet. Only family
Compensates. You must marry.

FREDERIK   Give up flowers
For one proliferating weed? Curtail
The wind's exuberance of roistering sport
Round bachelors who sail with wanton masts,
For the ducked head at breakfast, clay-cold
          sheets,
And, from the street at dawn, the lifted foot
Into the creaking door of poor excuse?

MAURITS   If you won't, I shall have to marry. Legitimize
My Margaretha's children. See! Dusk falls
Across my day. Stand here, and make your
          choice.

FREDERIK   That would deprive me of all I have dreamed,
Lived for, and aimed at: to emulate you,
And honour your creation of this country
By guiding it across fresh-blowing seas.
Who else has the experience? Not your sons!

MAURITS   I tell you: make your choice!

FREDERIK   I can't be faithful!

MAURITS   Answer me, blast your hull! I have no time
Left now. The sand has run. Give me your
          choice!

FREDERIK   Is this how one should make loving selection

For life, for children and posterity?
I will not have some unknown cabbage-Frau,
Who at the climax of her pleasure cracks
A nut, or eats an apple, foisted on me
For ugly duty or plain politics!
Well, if I must, I'll wed the girl I bed
Just at this moment: Amalia of Solms-Braunfels.

MAURITS   Good! Lady-in-waiting to the Queen
Elizabeth of Bohemia. You have taste –
You always had: and you will build a court
To rival France and dazzle Europe! I
Am most relieved I do not have to marry.
Nothing raises one's spirits more. You've cured
My empty silence with your wedding bell.

FREDERIK   Now I'm the snail scorched lifelong to his shell!

                 Fade.

                        SCENE FIVE

                 The Speelhouse. ISICIATA, SAPPHO *and* LESBIA.
                 *Music : Handel, 'Ottone', Act II: duet, Gismonda
                 and Matilda 'Notte cara, a te si deve'.*

SAPPHO   Rembrandt is married!

LESBIA   And he brings his bride
                 Round here to introduce her.

SAPPHO   Who is she?

ISICIATA   His dealer's cousin: Saskia. An orphan,
                 Youngest child of eight – the Uylenburghs.
                 They say she's twenty-one, now.

LESBIA   And a beauty?

ISICIATA   We'll see. I know she brings a dowry,

                                          Though not how much.

LESBIA   If she has seven sisters
                              It won't go far.

SAPPHO   I hope she likes us!

ISICIATA   Make
                              Her welcome. Let her talk. Don't flirt with
                                    Rembrandt.
                              A new bride's left old friends, so make her feel
                              The happy centre of attention here.

LESBIA   Break her in.

SAPPHO   Now, now!

ISICIATA   I have found it's best
                              If a sweet, friendly girl of her own age
                              Clearly enjoying herself, healthy and fresh ...

SAPPHO   Like you, my Lesbia!

LESBIA   Sappho! Just like you!

ISICIATA   Takes her aside and shows her all the fun.

SAPPHO   No! Leave her to her bridegroom! We'll be
                                    friends,
                              And find out what she's like.

LESBIA   If Rembrandt loves her
                              She must be good in bed, and easy-natured ...

ISICIATA   They're here!

                  Enter REMBRANDT *and* SASKIA *with a wrapped up
                  painting.*

REMBRANDT   Sorry we're late.

ISICIATA   You've brought the
                              painting!

LESBIA   Oh I can't wait to see how you have smoothed
                Our shivering bodies in your studio
                Into the shimmering sunlight of your brush!

SAPPHO   You didn't paint her spots?

LESBIA   What do you mean!

SASKIA   Hullo! I'm Saskia.

ISICIATA   We welcome you! *(Kisses her)*

SAPPHO   (SAPPHO *and* LESBIA *each take her arm*)
                Come, sit between us as we see unveiled
                All Frederik Hendrik asked for.

SASKIA   He comes here?

ISICIATA   He asked your husband to create from these
                Two girls, who served him, Sappho and Lesbia,
                A scene from Ovid's *Metamorphoses*
                To hang up in his bedroom. Rulers should
                Know how we common people think, and
                              laugh ...

LESBIA   And love!

ISICIATA   He's our most honoured guest; eats
                              here
                When he's back from the wars, to meet the
                              artists.

LESBIA   And drinks.

ISICIATA   When Frederik Hendrik comes to
                              power
                We'll have a Prince all of us can admire.

LESBIA   Show us transmuted and immortalized!

ISICIATA   Lead into gold.

SASKIA   *(Laughing)* No, no! You can't
          say that:
          You two are pretty!

LESBIA   Listen, Saskia:
          We love you. Say it again?

SASKIA   You are fresh and
          healthy.

          ISICIATA, SAPPHO *and* LESBIA *exchange meaningful
          glances.*

LESBIA   We are your friends for life.

SASKIA   Show us the canvas!
          He's hidden it from me until it's finished.
          What's it about? I know it tells a story ...

ISICIATA   First, *(To* SAPPHO*)* pour some bright wine in a
                    long-blown glass
          For each of us.

REMBRANDT   Saskia, sit on my lap.

LESBIA   Let's stick this hat on him, so that he looks
          A laughing bachelor with playful lady.

SASKIA   His favourite fantasy – a purchased woman.
          Oh, I'm enjoying this. I'll drink to me!
          (SASKIA *is sitting on* REMBRANDT*'s lap*)
          Now, lover-husband: ready? Show, and explain.

LESBIA   Sappho read out the legend to us while
          We posed, goose-bumped and waiting.

SASKIA   Sappho, tell
                    all!
                    (Show slide no. 6, of Rembrandt: 'The Goddess
                    Diana bathing, Acteon, and Callisto's Pregnancy
                    discovered' (1634) Bredius 472. Anholt, Museum
                    Wasserburg Anholt, Germany)

SAPPHO   Look! There we are! Diana's wanton nymphs,
                    Playful and naked, bathe beneath a tree
                    Unabashed in delight. Wet to her thighs
                    This ducks her friend to expose to our eyes
                    Her friend's round bottom. All have shed their
                              clothes
                    But ripe Callisto, with the darker hair,
                    And one, behind, turbaned, who pinions her.
                    Five girls, bare, sun-warmed, crowd Callisto
                              while
                    Miss Turban pulls her back, down. Two hold
                              her arm
                    Lest she be modest, while Beauty in front –
                    A kneeling, coiffured, golden nude – takes
                              charge,
                    As gripped Callisto tries to cross her thighs,
                    Pushes her dress up navel-high to hold,
                    Feel where we came from, and to give her
                              pleasure,
                    See if she is a virgin – finds she's pregnant!
                    A sixth stands shameless, throwing her hair
                              back, laughing,
                    Pointing to poor Callisto now revealed
                    As having broken Dian's virgin law
                    For which she will be turned into a bear.

LESBIA   For being unchaste? The world will be a zoo!

SASKIA   It's wonderful! I can see which is you,
                    Lesbia.

SAPPHO   Yes, by her bottom.

SASKIA   *(Laughing)* No; by her
                    laugh!
          Sappho, is that you pushing up her dress?

REMBRANDT   All are transformed for the Prince Frederik
                    Hendrik,
          And he'll appreciate his leisure friends
          Lit by his bedside candles. Lesbia, Sappho,
          Thank you for posing; for your friendly welcome
          To Saskia, my bride.

SASKIA   We live so close,
          Why, we can eat here often.

LESBIA   As he used to.

SASKIA   Nothing need change! A newly-married girl
          Needs friends of her own sex. I do love wine
          In merry company!

REMBRANDT   *(Aside to* SAPPHO, *who is looking at* SASKIA *with
          undisguised lust)*
                            Sappho, she's mine.
          For you I'll paint her as a Venus, thrilled
          As I approach her on our bridal night,
          So you can see all you want: but don't touch!

SASKIA   *(Climbing back on* REMBRANDT *'s lap)* My love,
                    paint me, here, sitting on your lap,
          As a late wedding present.

REMBRANDT   Yes, I shall. *(Kisses her.*
          Others applaud. Show slide no. 7, of Rembrandt:
          'Rembrandt and Saskia' (1635 – 1636) Bredius 30.
          Dresden, Gemäldegalerie. To ISICIATA*)*
          And you need something over the fireplace
                    there.
          What's it to be? From Ovid?

SAPPHO   Ganymede;

To celebrate the love that cannot breed.

*Music : Handel, 'Ottone', Act II: duet, Gismonda
and Matilda 'Notte cara, a te si deve'.*

Fade.

SCENE SIX

TRIGLAND *and* SMOUT.

TRIGLAND

Predikant Adrianus Smout, substantial
Colleague; isn't it reassuring to
Drink in, savour this scent, that in five minutes
We will be standing on the other side
Of that door *(Indicating invisible fourth wall
between them and audience)* being effortlessly
     charming?
How are you?

SMOUT

(Tapping his large stomach) Well, you know what
     it is, Trigland.
I've a soft spot for mushrooms with my meat.
Even the smell of fungi in a wood
After rain, before breakfast, brings saliva
Of praise to the rumble of gratitude.

TRIGLAND

               True hunger
Of holy thought: but, dear Smout, can you buy
Mushrooms this time of year?

SMOUT

            Ah, Jacobus!
In the city we choose our own friends:
In a village they are forced on us.
Not in the fields, but here in Amsterdam
There is a darkened shed where I can choose –
Alone, in secret – soft and shell-like growths:
Cut their stems low and drop them in my
     bucket;

Or feel the huge, white semi-globes, too big
For any stem to lift them. Others, shameless,
Circumcised, waving moonlit in their stink
Proud and triumphant, are pulled from their
    rags
Perfumed on slatted shelves in thick manure,
To beautify my fork.

TRIGLAND   I know that shed
Where vegetation reprobate 's confined
And women may not go: it's been destroyed.

SMOUT   My ruminating shed, where I correct,
As His priest, nature's dirty jokes for God
While meditating on the *Song of Songs?*

TRIGLAND   Some sons of Belial, in clogs, stamped on
The gathered produce of a day's hard work,
Chanting songs lacking in sublimity:
Riot – set off by plague, and execution
Of sailors hired by sons of Barnevelt
To kill Prince Maurits on a mistress-visit.

SMOUT   We shall proclaim in the Consistory
That burgomasters and town councillors
Who allow heretic Arminians,
Slackly, to get away with blasphemy
Should be trans-shipped across the river Y
To public gallows to stare at the stars
Through loops, well-knotted, of strong
        hempen rope.

TRIGLAND   Let's visit churches throughout Holland to
Unite against weak magistrates who leave
Arminian moderates, children of perdition,
Unpunished when – against our new-pressed
    laws
Forbidding meetings of Remonstrance
        Church –
They defy and ignore, meet, write and build.

SMOUT

Our Lord told us to love our enemies,
But no, not those who ought to be our friends.
These first-shoots of foul Anti-Christ, the spawn
Of Satan, children of the Dragon, where
The Whore of Babylon sits on the Beast
With seven heads ...

TRIGLAND

                Yes! When I erred with Rome
No deviation from orthodoxy
Was tolerated by the Inquisition.
Spaniards smashed a Dutch bridal couple's door
And sliced the naked groom down at bare feet
Of his bride-widow, who reeled round in shock
To be torn from her pearls and underclothes,
From knees to neck exposed to lashing wounds
Out in the street. She ran. Another found
Her hiding place and gave, after some play,
The coup de grâce, throwing her corpse to rot.

SMOUT

We won Dutch freedom from that Spanish
      yoke
And Whore of Rome with blest simplicity
As Calvin's pastors shepherding our flock
Preaching beneath the oaks in peaceful fields,
Loved and revered by all. We must keep pure
Orthodox Calvinism: only one
Religion tolerated in the state.

TRIGLAND

There are too many Catholics to fine ...

SMOUT

Threaten them every year with rigour; but
Allow contrite donations to our funds
From the rich papist congregation, as
They cannot split us, and we cannot lose.

TRIGLAND

Just as we do with brothels, playhouses!
The Jesuits encourage Bible-plays
In schools and theatres ...

SMOUT

                To make a play

Of Holy Writ is profanation! Sin!

TRIGLAND   Our Consistory answers the Town Council
'Even if you will not enforce the laws ...

SMOUT   All heretics from our Dutch Reformed Church
Must be expelled to exile. The Lord says:
"Better a desolate city than a hub
Of empire teeming with sectarians."'

TRIGLAND   Our Sunday sermons will remind them all
The General Synod convened at Dordrecht
Affirmed the world's total depravity,
God's own elect, rationed atonement; and
Proclaimed Arminian heretics to be
Unfrocked, found guilty, banished or
        imprisoned,
To keep spring well of Calvinism clean.

SMOUT   *(To audience)* Come! Poor in spirit, children of
        the Lord!
If magistrates grow too slack to enforce
Law, blind-eyed burgomasters still neglect
Their duty to stamp out all heresy,
Take up these very cobbles underfoot;
Of these stones mould the bread of
        righteousness,
And when Arminian Oldenbarnevelts
Meet, near the tower of Montelbaan, defiant,
Paupers, you pillage law into your hands
To teach our senators divinity!

TRIGLAND   *(To audience)* Eight thousand bodies have died
        of the plague
This year in Amsterdam, eight thousand souls
Dispatched to judgement from foul-smelling
        dark
Of Amsterdam's corruption of God's word.
We threw off Rome for freedom's innocence,
And must not let the moderates in arts

And government split our society,
Toss all away!

SMOUT   All arts must serve the church;
But those that bring forth briars and thorns be
      burned.
Alas! This city, clothed in scarlet, decked
In purple with fine gold and precious stones,
Your merchants are the great men of the earth
Committing fornication with that Beast
Of Mammon, the Great Whore! Your smoke
      shall rise
As incense to the marriage of the Lamb,
And dogs, and sorcerers, and blasphemers
Be hurled from Holland – Catholics,
      Remonstrants,
Cartesians; all corrupt Calvin's milk.
Incensed by your obedience to Baal
Your dance around the Golden Calf is struck
By lightning from God's frown through us, his
      priests!

TRIGLAND   Those unelect who disagree are beasts.

SCENE SEVEN

REMBRANDT 's *workshop.*
REMBRANDT, LIEVENS, FABRITIUS *and*
HOOGSTRAETEN.

REMBRANDT   Yes, Pieter Lastman's ill. Now I'm in charge.
These two boys are my new apprentices:
Long-curly-haired Carel Fabritius –
With your wide-angle telescope, and love
Of double concave lenses! His father is
Precentor in his church; of course a painter,
But also the church sexton: useful for corpses.
And even younger than Fabritius
Is Samuel Hoogstraeten who's come to me

Because his father's been called up to heaven.
Both you unfocused sproutlings, you must spend
Less time on optical illusions, dreams
In trompe l'oeil, and three-dimensional
Models for churches we shall never build,
And prepare portraits for me that will sell!

LIEVENS   I've come to say 'Good-bye'. I leave for England;
Perhaps to paint the court and meet Van Dyck –
But I shall miss our master, Pieter Lastman,
And his obsessive plants, buildings, weapons,
Pots of gold and silver craftsmanship
Incongruously stuck in his crowd scenes!
Hoogstraeten, Rembrandt is your father now.
Fabritius, make the most of your time here.
Both of you, learn from Rembrandt to contrast
Heavy impasto with thin oil paint glaze
Driven by broad and fluctuating brushstrokes.
We've raced each other, but he wins the crown.

FABRITIUS   Yes, yes; I know all that, but let me bring
A little silver daylight to his gloom,
Shimmer some natural grace from out of doors,
While meadowed April wakens up the sky,
Against which sitters can be starkly seen.
(*To* HOOGSTRAETEN) Mind what you're doing with that clumsy sword!
Why do you wear it?

HOOGSTRAETEN   I'm a courtier poet!
I'll brush an image of me to the world
Complete with golden-chained medallion,
Spontaneous charm and princely courtesy –
That poetry of life lived gracefully.
What says Michaelangelo? 'Every painter
Paints his own likeness best.' Look what I've made!

(HOOGSTRAETEN *shows his 'Perspective Box' (n.d.)*
London, National Gallery. Slide no. 8)
I'm fascinated by tricks of perspective,
Lievens. See through this open side. All's flat?
The chairs, that flat dog painted on ground
    and wall?
Look through this hole. The dog sits on the
    floor.

LIEVENS   Well! By my father's hatmaking and thimble,
Doors open out in views to other rooms,
The mirror tilts, the red chairs now stand
    clear!
A broom no longer than my finger looks
Solid and large as life! Fabritius,
What can you show me?

FABRITIUS   Well, more of the same:
(Show slide no. 9, of Carel Fabritius: 'View in Delft,
with a Musical Instrument Seller's Stall' (1652)
London, National Gallery)
A view in Delft, a man selling instruments,
Distorted to fit a perspective box
With back wall semi-circular. But, Lievens,
You know how Rembrandt took your 'Lazarus'
And raised Christ's arm, which you had clasped
    in prayer?
He never finished it; made a new etching;
But I have challenged you,
(Show slide no. 10, of Carel Fabritius: 'Raising of
Lazarus' (1643 – 6) Warsaw Museum Narodowe)
                   brought all the light
Out from the grave, up on the dead man's
    waking
Face.

HOOGSTRAETEN   He's coming up from hell all right,
Wonderful poses in your cheering crowd,
But only you would make Almighty God
So absent-minded he stares at dead feet.

REMBRANDT   The boy has talent. A large work like that,
               Lievens, you will agree, demands applause.
               The light's dramatic, and you've used my arm,
               Lowered a little. Next thing you must learn
               Is to relate the figures as a group,
               Not leave each isolated; then this act
               Revealing man as God deepens and binds,
               Shocks with its irrefutable command.
               *(Show slide no. 11, of Rembrandt: 'The Raising of
               Lazarus' (c. 1632) etching and burin, Schwartz,
               'Rembrandt's Etchings (1977)', Bartsch 73)*

FABRITIUS   Rembrandt! There are your drapes – and in a
                   cave!
               But undeniably this grips the heart.
               The Magdalen, lit with her chin above
               The light-shelled grave; her sister's at the foot
               Terrified, wanting to reach out, but cramped ...

HOOGSTRAETEN   Martha in shadow, and the hatted man
               Hurled back by resurrection. Christ is calm,
               A force of total faith destroying death!

REMBRANDT   Lievens, it all goes back to you.

LIEVENS   But we
               Learned from Pieter Lastman, ebbing now
               Under his waning star, how to call up
               A crowd from long past, shocked in amber as
               Drama with outstretched arms burns into canvas.

HOOGSTRAETEN   His *(Indicating* FABRITIUS*)* father dreaded a
                   corpse waking up.
               Rembrandt is so dramatic he would smear
               A ripe nude Cleopatra under 'taan' –
               That darkening shellac – to irradiate
               One pearl!

REMBRANDT   Lievens, you are our pearl, dear
                   friend.

Come back to Holland when King Charles's
    court
Clouds over. We have paced each other since
Our mid-teens. Vondel's stage groups learn
    from you.

LIEVENS   That tender playwright! I've a parting gift.
Keep this: my etching of our poet Vondel.
(Show slide no. 12, of Jan Lievens: 'Joost van den
Vondel' (c. 1644 – 50) etching, Amsterdam,
Rijksmuseum)
May he, and you, and your two virtuoso
Toccata players of ghostly perspective,
Eaglets of hatching immortality,
Find, in your Saskia's bridal harmony,
The full sail of fair winds.

FABRITIUS   Write to us soon,
Before full-bellied wink of the new moon! *(Fade)*

SCENE EIGHT

REMBRANDT *and* SASKIA.

REMBRANDT   Like a paused dragonfly over a pool
Of lilies on a warm day, Constantijn
Huygens leaves Court awhile to visit us.

SASKIA   Here? Now! Good! Is it true that he has written
Six hundred music pieces?

REMBRANDT   And has sung,
And played the lute to the late King of England,
James.

SASKIA   What contacts! He's your most efficient
Agent.

REMBRANDT   True: but Frederik Hendrik knows

His own mind, and discriminates.

SASKIA   My love;
What will you show him when he fills the room
With his shrewd, peacock personality?

REMBRANDT   I want him to see my most recent work.

SASKIA   Two tender portraits of me heavy-robed
With wilting flowers?

REMBRANDT   Only one droops in each!

SASKIA   *(Skittishly)* Me as patron saint of naughty
          women:
Flora, Rome's Queen of mercenary love!
In each of them you've shown me very
          pregnant.
Do you think he'll mind?

REMBRANDT   I love you full of life.
I'll show that Venus of you, when our son
Rombartus was just born, and you were resting
On the carved bed, with all the drapes drawn
          back ...

SASKIA   With you dressed (unlike me!), your hat on,
          creeping
In on our bridal night – except the sun
Clearly shines on a love-filled afternoon!
*(Show slide no. 13, of Rembrandt: 'Danae' (1636)
Bredius 474. St Petersburg, Hermitage)*

REMBRANDT   There I've brushstroked your stomach back to
          normal.

SASKIA   Fat.

REMBRANDT   And your palm's raised, head turned,
          welcoming.

I tried to see how Titian creamed his nudes,
But Leonardo's curve round your right thigh
Deflected me, made me preoccupied,
Wholly absorbed, to find what hidden thought,
What outward gesture of a woman's mind
Waiting her longed-for lover, in sunlight,
Bare in anticipation, shoes kicked off,
Might be discovered, brought out and
      revealed.

SASKIA   You have a generous view of all my lumps.
But, darling, why use that same trick of light
Through drapes for the most horrifying probe
An artist ever dreamed?

Enter HUYGENS.

HUYGENS   Friends! Opportune?
If not, I'll leave ...

SASKIA   No! Come in, Constantijn!
We hoped you'd find a moment to escape
Your world of politics.

HUYGENS   I sometimes think
That the most savage politics erupt
In the volcano of creation's heat:
The arts.

REMBRANDT   You speak with feeling.

HUYGENS   I've been hurt.

SASKIA   How, Constantijn?

REMBRANDT   Has my name brought you
      pain?

HUYGENS   No, no! Dear Rembrandt, I would champion
      you

Against kings with their armies. No. The muse
Of sacred music, Polyhymnia, spanked.

SASKIA   Who could dislike your playing of the lute,
                Or songs exquisite ravishing the ears
                Of all who hear them lifted on the breeze?

HUYGENS   No one, I hope. I learned that lute aged seven;
                And later, with my viol, in autumn dusks,
                Made evening music with my parents' friends
                In Johan Sweelinck's home. He started me,
                Aged ten, on his church organ, which I love!
                And, to stop organs being thrown out of
                    church
                Across this country, I have published – with
                Full, warm enthusiasm of our Prince –
                A treatise to defend those 'Popish Pipes'
                (That's what they call Cecilia's harmonies!)
                Pleading for lively organ accompaniments.

REMBRANDT   Bigoted Philistines! I've painted some.
                Look here. *(Show slide no. 14, of Rembrandt: 'The
                Blinding of Samson' (1636) Bredius 501.
                Frankfurt, Städelsches Kunstinstitut)*

HUYGENS   Rembrandt! That is just too much!

REMBRANDT   Delilah raping Samson of his strength:
                There's sex and violence probing my worst
                    fear.
                I want to understand our deepest thoughts;
                And most extreme emotions open up
                Windows into our being, richer far
                Than any objects. All I need's a face.

HUYGENS   You need not put a dagger through its eye!
                It's a titanic lightning-blast of glare
                On the curved blade that spurts the leaping
                    eye-ball;
                Appalling, as his fist and toes clench white,

In unevadable ferocity.
Ugh! What is that one?
(Show slide no. 15, of Rembrandt: 'Danae' (1636)
Bredius 474. St Petersburg, Hermitage) Oh yes: just
    a face?
Have you forgotten you painted her body?

REMBRANDT   They're the same curtains from our bed.

SASKIA   He's
    changed
The colours, slightly; thank God! I can't sleep
If he thinks that ...

HUYGENS   While you are feeling this!
Show me, before I go, one less extreme:
Saskia's portrait? (Is Delilah she?)

REMBRANDT   Of course; but here is Saskia as Flora.
(Show slide no. 16, of Rembrandt: 'Saskia as Flora'
(1635) Bredius 103. London, National Gallery)

HUYGENS   That's better! Was she ... I mean ... How's the
    babe?

SASKIA   Tiny Rombartus needs his feed soon. Yes,
My pregnant bulge is half-disguised in flowers.

HUYGENS   How sweet! How lovely! Decorous; gentle;
    smiling ...

REMBRANDT   Well, that's because I changed it in mid-paint
From Judith with the screaming severed head
Of Holofernes – covered that with flowers,
But left the old expression on her face.

SASKIA   I couldn't stand me as it was. I'm Flora!
(Confidentially) He loves to paint me as a
    prostitute;
And it excites me! *(Exit* SASKIA*)*

HUYGENS   Should I know all this?,
                    The frost of iron singes in your soul,
                    Rembrandt. Why?

REMBRANDT   Because our little son
                    Our darling baby, I know now, will die.

                    Blackout.

                    SCENE NINE

                    FREDERIK HENDRIK *and* HUYGENS. *Later*
                    REMBRANDT.

HUYGENS   Like a duet which tennis-balls a theme
                    Through smoothest serves, first to the left,
                        then right
                    In modulating, mounting counterpoint,
                    So these two friends, Lievens and Rembrandt,
                        test,
                    Compete against each other, cap returns,
                    Daring imagination raise the stakes
                    Till Rembrandt triumphs with sure, detailed
                        touch
                    Of caught emotion in a face, a gesture,
                    Eyes, woven interactions of a scene,
                    While Lievens taunts the more audacious
                        themes,
                    Vigorous and untamed, on a grand scale.

FREDERIK   Like autumn's swallow he leaves us awhile
                    To nest in England and to beard Van Dyck.
                    Since my dear brother Maurits, coughing gold,
                    Died, passing his responsibilities
                    As Captain-General of the Union
                    To me, I've been preoccupied with war.
                    Breda, our city-stronghold in the south
                    Was raped by that Italian banker thug
                    Spinola, lackey of Spain – dead now, thank
                        God! –

And I must pluck that Orange-Nassau home
From Philip's teeth, and leave him mouthing
    gums.
My state of Orange, too, in southern France,
Where summer's mist sets over ripened pears,
Catholic though it is, needs my defence.

HUYGENS   Send them, in reassurance – to remind
The State of Orange daily who's their Prince –
Altarpieces by Rembrandt. When all kneel
In holy reverence, they'll think of you.

FREDERIK   Splendid! That cannot compromise our
       Calvin
Here in the Dutch north. Show me
      Rembrandt's room.

HUYGENS and FREDERIK HENDRIK *enter and see*
REMBRANDT *painting.*

REMBRANDT   My Prince; for no one else would I have
      paused.

FREDERIK   What a magnificent self-portrait! Why,
(Show slide no. 17, of Rembrandt: 'Self-portrait'
(1640) Bredius 34. London, National Gallery)
You pose as Titian's 'Ariosto', with
Arm-resting, lordly ease, a courtier
Like Baldassare Castiglione ...

HUYGENS   Whom
Raphael portrayed. Rembrandt paints his claim
To be our 'Titian of the North'; and like
Great masters of the art in Italy
You sign now with one word, thumb-wrestling
    with
Painting's Grand-Master.

FREDERIK   Thank you for your
    deft

Mythologizing of our speelhouse girls
Into Diana and Callisto's friends:
Ovid delights the wit; lives in your light.

REMBRANDT   You are too busy and too mighty now
To share our speelhouse.

FREDERIK   Yes; and I have
changed.
Would you match Rubens, as you've challenged
Titian?
Some altarpieces for the south of France?

REMBRANDT   Why not ask Rubens?

FREDERIK   Three times he has been
My guest, as diplomat and enemy.
He is not welcome any more.

REMBRANDT   What themes?

HUYGENS   Remember Ruben's Antwerp altarpieces
At St. Walburga, and in the cathedral?
Outclass them! Paint a 'Raising of the Cross'
Paired with a 'Taking down of Our Lord's
Body'.

REMBRANDT   Their size?

HUYGENS   No, smaller: measurements you'll get.

FREDERIK   I've seen your etching of raised Lazarus,
And that is why I'm here.

REMBRANDT   It's for your Catholics
Down in unwintered France?

FREDERIK   My subjects there
Venerate Rome as we acknowledge Calvin;
The House of Orange must have room for all.

You need not compromise our own beliefs.

REMBRANDT   Mennonites talk more sense. The Catholics
        claim
The Virgin Mary's stoicism must
Be shown, for she who trusted God as wife
Would suffer patiently all that He willed,
Not flinching from the worst. As Protestant
I'll answer that and show her breaking heart,
Paint it with all the emotion in my power.

FREDERIK   Create as you will. There's no higher theme.
Become God's courtier as you paint the scene.
(Fade)

SCENE TEN

FREDERIK HENDRIK *and* HUYGENS.

FREDERIK   Where are you guiding me, my Hermes?

HUYGENS   On,
Clearing, like morning's breeze, night's
    ignorance
Away, showing you others whom you rule
Whose dreams are you might speak to them.

FREDERIK   I do!
You know my speelhouse friends, and all the
    artists!

HUYGENS   But there are others, educated, merchants,
Who look to you: protestants, yes, but not
Calvinists. Their hero is Erasmus.

FREDERIK   'Libertines' is the inapproprate name
They're given by all-condemning Smout, and
    Trigland.

HUYGENS   Liberals, but loyal. (Ignore fat Smout.)
                 One of them, our late Roemer Visscher, was
                 Corn-merchant ...

FREDERIK   And satiric poet! Mad
                 To purify our words to standard Dutch!

HUYGENS   Also caressed our shipping with insurance.
                 One Christmas Eve a cataclysmic storm
                 Sank twenty ships bellied with merchandise
                 Into the belching bottom of the sea
                 Off Texel – far in the north. He lost so much
                 That three months later, when his heavy wife
                 Brought to the crying daylight a new babe,
                 Their second daughter – whose house is right
                         here –
                 Maria, in a fit of wry self-pity
                 He nicknamed her Maria Tesselschade.
                 She swims, speaks fluent Latin, French, Italian,
                 And, much to my delight, plays the church
                         organ
                 In spite of the new ban.

                 FREDERIK HENDRIK *and* HUYGENS *enter* MARIA *'s
                 house.*

FREDERIK   What are you doing?

MARIA   Prince Frederik Hendrik, our own Stadholder!
                 (MARIA *curtseys*) Gratias tibi ago: non sum digna.

FREDERIK   Maria, all soft light the rainbow shakes
                 In dew that West Wind's blessing scatters on
                 The red anemone, Adonis' flower,
                 Picked by Persephone in Henna's field,
                 Rain down in bees' contentment through your
                         heart.

MARIA   Frederik Hendrik: as Proserpina
                 Wreathed flowers, and filled her laughing
                         osier-basket

                    Quite unsuspecting Pluto's chariot-rape,
                    You catch me unprepared to honour you
                    As you deserve.

HUYGENS   What are you making there?

MARIA   Diamond-point engraving on this glass.
              Can you read what I've carved?

FREDERIK   Please let me
                        try?
                    'A thaw on the freezing of love.' What froze
                        your heart?

MARIA   Pluto's chariot took my husband, daughter,
              Into the earth in the same day, and grave.
              All of a sudden they are gone.

HUYGENS   I have
              A poem for you, written when I heard.
              'There is no end to sorrow for one's blood,
              Those nearest to us; it runs everywhere:
              But words, though poor, don't bleed or fade.
                    For grief,
              What consolation is that? What relief?'

MARIA   Thank you, dear friend; and Frederik Hendrik,
                    you
              Visit me in my sadness. Thank you, sir.
              The only things that matter in this life
              Are acts of blessing and of pity.

FREDERIK   True;
              And yet how hard it is to live by that.
              My power is boxed in by the States General.
              I want to reunite the Netherlands
              But North will not protect the Catholic South.
              We must make war on Spain, or else make
                    peace.
              If war, take the offensive. A small state

Cannot remain defensive all the time.
The Calvinists support an active war
But will not tolerate Brabant as friend.
We must support our Church, but understand
Conscience, to prevent religious strife:
Dissent is health. Our State must include all,
And I will not lend soldiers to the Church,
Dutch troops, to torment Dutch integrity!

HUYGENS   Some fear your aim's a crown.

FREDERIK   Why should I want
            The dangerous trappings of a jealous title?
            Octavian showed strength grows with
                    disclaiming.
            Give others rank, reward, the laurel, triumphs;
            The power to make and break needs no such
                    thing.

MARIA   It is the kingmaker who rules the king.

Enter LESBIA *with bottle of red wine.*

LESBIA   I'm sorry, Madam.

MARIA   Lesbia! Yes, come in!
            This is the Prince, and Constantijn Huygens.

FREDERIK   We know each other, and my candles gleam
            On the bright humour of a Rembrandt scene
            Painted of Lesbia and her friends.

MARIA   High Prince.
            My husband, Allard Crombalgh, met me when
            He lurched the seas as a ship's officer.
            After we married he remained on land,
            A Regent of the Alkmaar poorhouses.

HUYGENS   With licence on the brothels.

MARIA
                                               Yes. She works
Part-time for me as dressmaker.

HUYGENS
                                              Polite
Employment on the side? Whatever next,
Lesbia! Did you know the Prince has paid
For a fine copy, for your speelhouse wall,
Of Dirck van Baburen's 'Procuress'? Yes,
Come and collect it when you will.

LESBIA
                             (Curtseys) Thank you. *(Exit)*

HUYGENS   Maria, I too grieve; a widower.
Susanna died in May.

MARIA
                                  I know.

HUYGENS
                                             If you
Would marry me, and Lesbia worked for both,
Neither of us need ever break our oath!

MARIA   *(Amused)* Maria Magdalena is the proof
God forgives sins, and breaks the chain of
        pearls.
The shadow on the meadow fades with youth.
But, naughty friend, three into two won't go!

MARIA *pours red wine into engraved glass and gives
it to* FREDERIK HENDRIK.

FREDERIK   Maria Tesselschade: all my thanks; *(Drinks)*
And may your glass engraving be your soul's
Mirror, transparent clarity that's wise;
Wine to the heart, perfection to the eyes.

MARIA   I fought the wish to die before God called,
And won. My enemy, with his grey scythe,
Retreated. Constantijn: harvest your grief
Into a book which will remember it
On your behalf. My Prince, dear friend of all

Your varied flock, we'll answer when you call.
As our Dutch garden ripens, now we're free,
You shake ripe plums of generosity
Down on us all, sheltered beneath your tree.
(Fade)

SCENE ELEVEN

MARIA. *To her* TRIGLAND *and* SMOUT.

TRIGLAND   May we come in? You know for whom we
                speak.

MARIA   The Consistory; yes. I'm not prepared.

TRIGLAND   But we are, Maria Crombalgh. We both know
            You have been visited by Frederik Hendrik.

MARIA   He, and my friend Constantijn Huygens left
         Just now.

TRIGLAND   We saw; and that is why we're here.
            The Stadholder is tolerant of Rome.

MARIA   He is a Calvinist.

TRIGLAND   In public, yes;
            But toleration of the Catholics

SMOUT   And others ...

TRIGLAND   Shows a fundamental weakness.

SMOUT   And we hear rumours that the Church of
                Rome
         Begins, like a seductive, smiling harlot,
         To beckon, pull you!

MARIA   Why do you say this?

TRIGLAND   Because your friend the poet Vondel is
                No longer Baptist but a howling Papist ...

SMOUT   Spread-eagled on the seven hills of Rome
                Where cardinals like ants gnaw at his soul.
                Have you imagined rape?

MARIA   *(Startled)* I am a widow.

SMOUT   I ask for reasons theological.
                That sulphur-smelling father of their church
                Thomas Aquinas teaches Catholics
                That masturbation is far worse than rape
                Because God-given seed is wholly wasted.

TRIGLAND   Did you know that? Better to rape than spill?
                A Catholic doctrine?

MARIA   Tell me what you think.

TRIGLAND   Johannes Calvin teaches that the Fall
                Is partially redeemed by marriage vows.
                Whatever sin or shame is in the act
                Of procreation is subsumed between
                Husband and wife in mutual delight.

SMOUT   As we can see in Solomon's great song
                On which I've made a commentary in verse.

TRIGLAND   And therefore if a man should choose a wife

SMOUT   Because of her round breasts ...

TRIGLAND   her elegance
                Of shape will not, necessarily, sin.

MARIA   That's a relief.

SMOUT   So the Old Testament
                Calls up the bridal chamber of the king:

'Let him kiss me with the kisses of his mouth,
For thy love is better than wine.'

MARIA   Does Calvin comment on this?

TRIGLAND   Smoutius does.

SMOUT   'Thy lips are a thread of scarlet,
Thy neck's hung with shields and bucklers.'

TRIGLAND   A necklace.

SMOUT   'Thy breasts are like two fawns' (Leaping
                    about)
That feed among the lilies.' (Need I explain?)

MARIA   No; you need not: but you will.

SMOUT   Lilies: teats.
'Until the daylight breaks and shadows flee
I will get me to the mountain of myrrh.'
We're going down her body, as you see,
'Mountain of myrrh', the pungent *mons veneris*.

MARIA   Are these songs that you teach your
                    congregation?

TRIGLAND   He is about to try.

MARIA   I'd be embarrassed
And ashamed to sing them.

SMOUT   You were married!
Concupiscence and lust must be controlled,
Diverted into holy intercourse
Whose end is Christian children.

TRIGLAND   Otherwise
Female lust will undermine the state
And call down God's curse as the dikes collapse!

MARIA   Gentlemen; I have listened, as you wished,
To carnal words distasteful to someone
Who thinks refinement is to understand
What it must feel like to be listening.
God gave to everyone a conscience;
And freedom, which we prize, must honour
     this.

TRIGLAND   The Government connives at Popery;
Lends armed support to crush the Huguenots ...

MARIA   Predikants, there is nothing I can do
To change this. *(Church bell rings)* I must kneel
     now in my pew.

                Exeunt.

SCENE TWELVE

REMBRANDT *and* SASKIA.

SASKIA   How do you deal with grief?

REMBRANDT   I paint.

SASKIA   I can't.
What can unnumb grief's bleeding womb of
     loss,
Pull the tears back into the red-rimmed eyes
To soothe them into laughter once again?
What cure for cuddled blankets with no form?
For weight of sadness in the breasts? You've lost
Your mother. She was old and mine was young,
Yet they still bore us, and leave vacancy;
But a new baby ...

REMBRANDT   Saskia. You asked
Why I painted alone so much. *(Lifting picture on
     to easel)* For you!

Our home, set as a 'Holy Family'.
(Show slide no. 18, of Rembrandt: 'The Holy Family'
(1635) Bredius 544. Munich, Alte Pinakothek)
That's why I sketched him dying, to record
Our first-born happiness before it left.

SASKIA   Oh, love! Yes, I was wondering if I
Should cut his toe-nails. You had plumped his
          pillow;
His sleeping mouth's just fallen from my nipple.
Thank you, dear love.

REMBRANDT   I gave it all I had.
May I paint you?

SASKIA   Now I've lost weight? Am ill?

REMBRANDT   Just one more portrait of my joy; and hope.

SASKIA   My darling. Then, as in those dawn-song days
When all was young, make me your courtesan
Once more.

REMBRANDT   I'll model it on Titian's 'Flora',
His courtesan who offers us a flower.
(Show slide no. 19, of Titian: 'Flora' (c. 1515)
Florence, Uffizi)

SASKIA   But cover up my breasts. They sag, although
I'm not yet thirty.

REMBRANDT   Love!

SASKIA   Though you may like
          them,
Remember all the copies that will sell,
Done by your students.

REMBRANDT   I can shape them
          young.

SASKIA   Live by your own words: 'Always tell the truth
In paint, down to the smallest wrinkle.' That's
What makes you tower above all Amsterdam!
Don't compromise integrity for me
And lose your soul.

SCENE THIRTEEN

Enter VONDEL.

VONDEL   The door was open, friends.
Saskia! Rembrandt!

SASKIA   Ah! Dear Vondel, we
Need your wise wings over our shadowed nest.

VONDEL   I've come to cheer you both – see the work done
On my *Palamedes*.

REMBRANDT   Play after play
Of yours I illustrate: Joseph, in Egypt,
In your translation, warning all who rule:
Sophompaneas; and your opening play
For our first theatre in Amsterdam
Gijsbrecht van Aemstel, which the Calvinists
Stopped on the first night as some enemy
Proclaimed that you would celebrate the Mass
On stage! It's set one mediaeval Christmas!
And, of course, your *Palamedes*.

VONDEL   I'm fined
For writing that. You'd better hide your canvas.

REMBRANDT   By whom?

VONDEL   The Hague.

REMBRANDT   What! Over Amsterdam's
Authority?

VONDEL   That's what our magistrates
Said. Ours tried me.

REMBRANDT   Who was the chief
           'Schepen'?

VONDEL   Strange to relate, Albert Koenaadts Burgh.

REMBRANDT Why, he suggested it!

VONDEL   Shh! Yes, he fined me
           Three hundred florins.

REMBRANDT   Scourging you with fox-
           tails!

VONDEL   And, as I left, paid me the fine himself.
           I am a Catholic, now.

REMBRANDT   So rumour goes.
           What made you take this step?

VONDEL   Just sudden death.

REMBRANDT Why, death is all around us! Saskia's pregnant,
           Suffers, and worries me – say I were left
           Without her, whom I love? With a small baby?
           Our Pieter Lastman's dead. You know our
                 griefs ...
           Consuming guilt, cramping each second
                 thought,
           And the vast emptiness small humans leave.
           If the Creator of the Universe –
           Think of the distance in between the stars;
           Of Africa; the oceans; Arctic wastes;
           Sun, burning lost savannahs of the sky –
           If He, who made all this, chose to shrink down
           To visit us, and we nail-tortured Him
           To death, jeering, what hope is there for me?
           Judas is each of us. I don't have words.

Here I am: Rembrandt crucifying Christ.
(Show slide no. 20, of Rembrandt: 'The Raising of
the Cross' (1633?) Bredius 548. Munich, Alte
Pinakothek)

SASKIA   Huygens has bought it for Prince Frederik
                    Hendrik.
                Why do you cry?

VONDEL   Do you know why I came?

REMBRANDT   Your wife has died.

VONDEL   Yes. Mayke. She came back
                In bedside moonlight, telling me: 'Don't mourn.'
                You two have lost your child. Now, so have I.

SASKIA   Not Sara?

REMBRANDT   The little eight-year-old? Oh, no!

VONDEL   I can't paint Christ to show my heartbreak's
                    guilt;
                But let me, in my own poor way, share grief
                And utter loneliness. Friend, read for me.
                (VONDEL hands REMBRANDT his poem)

REMBRANDT   *(Reads)* 'Laughing Death, the lightning's Queen,
                Leaves white hairs to intervene
                    In a home to strike its joy.
                Every mother sheds black tears
                When a father's darkest fears
                    See the thunderbolt destroy.

                Here a little girl was playing
                With her friends, all holidaying
                    Endlessly, as is their right
                Before life demands attention
                Quite beyond their comprehension
                    In their early springtime's light.

There she swings, and shares a game,
Dancing, clapping, each nickname
    Sing-song called in quick delight
To chase on the hoop with bells
Rolled by sticks, while cockleshells
    Round her neck seem to take flight.

Her clear cheeks glow radiant
As tusks of an elephant
    Walk small Sara's feet as stilts.
She is happy, nor would change
Anything – just rearrange
    Mother's patchwork curtain-quilts.

Dolls are brought in from the stable
Till upon the kitchen table
    She picks up a chicken's claw
And by pulling on the muscle
In a concentrated tussle
    Makes it grip and lift once more.

But the dark Queen's touch turns frightening,
Loving trust is felled by lightning,
    Death's old game has kissed young lips.
All the mourners round her coffin
Dampen her last dress of muslin,
    Weep the child no longer skips.

"Would that we, not she, had died!"
Sobs each mourner. "We have tied
    In a garland green and gold
Flowers woven with no art,
Only bitter grief of heart
    To crown your soft brow so cold.'"

Fade.

SCENE FOURTEEN

TRIGLAND *and* SMOUT. *To them* VONDEL.

TRIGLAND Remonstrant moderates subvert the State
As well as God's decree. Toleration
Has gone too far. No lasting government
Has ever authorized free exercise
Of all sects and pretend-religious groups,
Even when they keep silent, and avoid
All politics. 'He that is not with us
Conspires against us' as Our Saviour says.

SMOUT The rooting out of bindweed heresy
With spade and pronged fork of anathema
And public condemnation is a task
Necessary in God's Calvin-patch ...

Enter VONDEL.

TRIGLAND Ah, poet Vondel! You look ill today.

VONDEL Thank you.

SMOUT And yet, with all the triumph of
Your publication of your poems ...

TRIGLAND Ah,
Your first *Collected* poems ...

SMOUT You should be
Elated and content!

VONDEL Perhaps.

TRIGLAND Is it
That, beautiful as is the printed work
With papist Sandrart's flattering frontispiece,
The book is not what it claims?

VONDEL   What do you mean?
                    If you look at the end you'll see I list
                    The longer works – the dramas – I omit.

SMOUT   Indeed you do: and what you do not say
                    Is that you have left out your finest verse.

VONDEL   My finest verse?

TRIGLAND   Oh, yes. Your poem made,
                    Magnificently, on the murder of
                    That King of France, the Bourbon Henri IV,
                    Who gave French Protestants full toleration:
                    Assassinated by François Ravaillac.
                    'This monstrous fruit grows from the poisoned
                        seed
                    The Whore of Babylon sows in the world ...'
                    Remember?

VONDEL   I do state my immature,
                    Young, adolescent, slight ephemera
                    Are better left forgotten ...

SMOUT   All attacks
                    On Catholics are missing.

VONDEL   You'd have me
                    Reprint rubbish discarded thirty-seven
                    Years ago?

SMOUT   But poetry endures!
                    Collected Poems should be what it claims.
                    (Sorrowfully) Now Rome has claimed your soul
                        you grow dishonest.

TRIGLAND   So, knowing all your past integrity,
                    And to protect your present reputation,
                    We have brought out your second volume ...

                    (Hands book to VONDEL*)*

VONDLE   What!

SMOUT   Of all you had left out from Volume One.
                 (Show slide no. 21, of Joachim Sandrart: Frontispiece
                 of Joost van den Vondel, 'Poëzy'. Amsterdam 1644)

TRIGLAND   We sweated, for your sake, through candlelight's
                 Old dusty papers many an owl-brushed night
                 To save you from disgrace; humiliation.
                 (Placing a friendly arm around VONDEL*'s shoulders)*
                 You have become a Roman Catholic;
                 And, as so often happens, this reveals
                 An aberration in your judgement. To
                 Prevent you telling untruth in your title,
                 Your being exposed, discredited, before
                 The world, thank your admirers for rescue
                 From such disgrace and consequent contempt.
                 Restoring truth we save your reputation.

VONDEL   A second volume: of all I discarded!
                 Worse still, without the dates when they were
                     written!
                 You make my journey home to Mother Church
                 Demonstrably, grotesquely, insincere.

SMOUT   Revenge is not our motive: love of truth.

VONDEL   You have defaced my life's work with my youth.

                 Fade.

                         SCENE FIFTEEN

                 REMBRANDT *and* SASKIA.

SASKIA   I'm cold. Please would you rock the cradle,
                     gently?

REMBRANDT   What did the doctors say?

SASKIA   Oh! Were they doctors?
I thought they were art-dealers, so I asked them
If Rubens' wife, Helena, whom we see
Tossed in the air, nude, in a thousand paintings
Were truly beautiful and richly dressed:

REMBRANDT   And they said?

SASKIA   I'm embarrassed.

REMBRANDT   'Not so fine
As you are, though much wealthier.' They're
          right!

SASKIA   I don't know why, but those words really
                    cheered me.
I feel Helena Rubens is my rival.
The art world's eyes look first on her, then me.

REMBRANDT   Copies of my portraits of you sell in dozens!

SASKIA   Yes. She has Europe's palace walls.

REMBRANDT   Saskia;
At sixteen, when he married her, she was
Vast: fifty-four inch hips, a double-chin,
Built large and meaty like a Flemish mare.
However many times he paints her naked
She's never nude: utterly passion-quelling.

SASKIA   Love, am I still provocative? Perhaps
You would not pay much for me now.

REMBRANDT   My love,
Nothing less than my whole world.

SASKIA   You love me?
Come here, and pay me richly, with your kiss.
You didn't marry just your dealer's cousin?
Or out of pity for my funny mouth?

My leaves are falling. If I could just once,
Hear the ripe acorns, like large drops of rain,
Fall in the sun, startling the moles and rabbits,
To be crunched underfoot; see shadowed trunks
Hold the wild eyebright, or Parnassus grass –
That lonely buttercup, but white – between
Their roots; if I could have the simple strength
To dry our baby Titus on my lap
After his bath; oh dearest –

REMBRANDT   Saskia!
Don't go! No! Saskia! No! No!

Quick fade, then show slide no 22, of Rembrandt:
'Saskia with a Flower' Bredius 108. Dresden,
Gemäldegalerie.

SCENE SIXTEEN

The Speelhouse. SAPPHO *and* LESBIA.
Music : Handel, 'Ottone', Act II: duet, Gismonda
and Matilda 'Notte cara, a te si deve'.

SAPPHO   Rembrandt's been left with just a tiny boy!

LESBIA   Do you think he'll manage?

SAPPHO   We shall have to
          help him,
As we are only minutes from his house.
I sometimes wish we had a baby here.
The trouble is, what with contraception,
And one seed driving out another, soon
Our bodies lose their pollen ...

LESBIA   A good thing
Our bodies grow less fertile!

Enter REMBRANDT.

Rembrandt! Oh
We wanted you to come and talk to us
About it all.

SAPPHO   Because we're here to help.
I know a girl who might nursemaid your Titus:
Widow of a ship's trumpeter from Hoorn,
But young; and she's broadminded.

REMBRANDT   What's her
       name?

SAPPHO   Geertge Dircx.

REMBRANDT   Bring her for interview.

LESBIA   We've hung your 'Ganymede' above the fire:
Opposite Dirck Baburen's, from the Prince.

REMBRANDT   His gets the better light!

SAPPHO   We've had it painted
By a young man from Delft, friend of Vermeer
Whom he will bring to see us!

REMBRANDT   What's his name?

SAPPHO   Pieter de Hoogh.
*(Show slide no. 23, of Pieter de Hoogh: 'Brothel with
Painting of Ganymede' (1663 – 5) Lisbon, Museu
Nacional de Arte Antiga)*
                    Look! He's recorded us
With your new 'Ganymede' up there in place!

REMBRANDT   Let me look closer.
*(Show slide no. 24, of Rembrandt: 'The Abduction of
Ganymede' (1635) Bredius 471. Dresden,
Gemäldegalerie)*

LESBIA   Tell me: why is he pissing?

REMBRANDT   Well; wouldn't you?

SAPPHO   To put the fire out.

REMBRANDT   All
Young children do.

SAPPHO   You should know!

REMBRANDT   I have
brought
A drawing of you, pen on brown, I sketched
For Saskia when she was ill, and missed
Your laughter and your music. Isiciata
Will, I hope, like the fact that here she's young?
(Show slide no. 25, of Rembrandt: 'The Prodigal
Son' (1635) Drawing, pen and wash. Frankfurt,
Städelsches Kunstinstitut)

SAPPHO   She's sitting at the table. Lesbia plays ...

LESBIA   No, *you* are playing. I'm being entertained!

REMBRANDT   Can't you tell by the faces? *(Lifts his picture)*
Help me, Sappho.
Much, much too late, I know, I can reveal
My promised glimpse for your wished fantasy.
(Show slide no. 26, of Rembrandt: 'Danae' (1636)
Bredius 474. St Petersburg, Hermitage)

SAPPHO   How wonderful! And yet, how very strange
To see a beauty sexually aware,
Whom we know, when she's lying in her grave
In our old church! I've lusted her so long,
Yet now I see all that I longed to stroke,
I want to tuck her in, and bring her soup
Before she catches cold.

LESBIA   Ripe; picked; and
rotting.

64   *Act One*

REMBRANDT   Ah! Botticelli painted Simonetta
             Nude after she was dead. Everything's changed
             To feelings too unbearable to share.

SAPPHO   Thank you for showing me. I think I'm cured.
             You look so lost ...

REMBRANDT   My dealer, Uylenburgh
             Has dropped me: not my dealer anymore.

LESBIA   But why? And what a time to be so vicious –
             And he is Saskia's relative!

SAPPHO   But why?

REMBRANDT   Some rows. I took over a year to paint
             'The Nightwatch' (as they call it) for the
                   Group
             From Precinct Two under Frans Banning Cocq.
             The light shines on him; but it shines on you,
             (*To* SAPPHO. *Show slide no. 27, of Rembrandt: 'The
             Company of Frans Banning Cocq preparing to
             March Out, known as The Nightwatch' (1642)
             Bredius 410. Amsterdam, Rijksmuseum*)
             Too. Yes I stuck you in as a young girl.
             Some do not like it; portrait faces hidden,
             And so on. Then another row; with Andries
             De Graeff, who said he'd pay five hundred
                   guilders
             For me to paint his portrait, which I've done:
             And now he does not want it and won't pay.

LESBIA   Leave this to us. When we have men like that
             We know just what to do. Shall we go round ...?

REMBRANDT   No, please! Where did you learn?

LESBIA   I started here
             In my mid-teens. No, I was not a servant.
             A seamstress; and when Isiciata sent

For extra girls, say when the ships came in
From the East Indies laden with spice and men,
She'd send a message, and I'd help her out.
How could I buy my clothes without her credit?

REMBRANDT   And you?

SAPPHO   I worked in a tobacco shop.
When Isiciata came to buy some pipes
She was her charming self. I needed help
As a boyfriend had just abandoned me.
She asked how much I earned. I told. 'You can
Make a week's wages in one night with me,
And have more fun – and food and drink for
     free.'

LESBIA   What other girls are painted by you artists?
All the creative people in this city
Come here at some point. Wives, to keep them
     young,
Bring older husbands to us for their birthday
Gift and treat; eat pancakes while they wait;
Drink, and hear music for which we are famed:
A good Dutch custom. (Not for Calvinists.
Why, they will spoil all the old ways!)

SAPPHO   We'll sing
Our love-song to each other to delight
And ravish all your sadnesses away.

LESBIA   I'll wisp your hair about those cheeks
       Fresh as a virgin's lip,
Till passing air turns back to look
       And lift each modest tip.
         Then in
         A plait
Weave round your crown a hive with pearls
     inlaid
Piled high to cage in curls the wind that
     played.

SAPPHO   Your nipple's shadow on its mound
                      Like an inverted mushroom
              Upon an upturned bowl of snow
                      When played with makes its flush bloom.
                              Such full
                              And proud
              Twin beauties turn the desert damp veined
                      blue
              When sunlight steals your privacy to view.

LESBIA   Your slender side's soft as a plum,
                      Your stomach's moon is junket
              With nutmeg freckled, like the cream
                      Before the cat has drunk it;
                              But ah!
                              Beyond
              There is a secret garden with one rose
              Arched by stray cobweb clouds where pleasures
                      doze.

SAPPHO   Your moulded thighs and graceful legs
                      Your slender tapered ankle
              If seen by other, plainer girls
                      Will make their envy rankle;
                              So hide
                              For me
              All save your footprints where, in the warm
                      grass,
              Violets twine and cuddle as you pass.

LESBIA   Now you must go and feed your baby, Titus.

REMBRANDT   A student's looking after him.

SAPPHO   *(Looking fondly at Rembrandt)* Dear man!

REMBRANDT   Thank you, good friends, for your kind
                      company.
              Saskia's laugh comes back to me with yours,
              Lifting my sadness, though she's under clay.

SAPPHO   Come! I'll look after you. You need not pay.
               (SAPPHO *drags* REMBRANDT *off*)

REMBRANDT   I'd like to ... *(Exeunt)*

               Show slide no. 28, of Rembrandt: 'Joseph and Potiphar's Wife' (1634) etching; Schwartz, 'Rembrandt's Etchings', Bartsch 39.

               Fade this slide into slide no. 29, Rembrandt: 'The Widower' – Man trying to feed Smiling Baby – Copenhagen, Statens Museum for Kunst, O. and E. Benesch 'The Drawings of Rembrandt' 1973, London and New York, Vol. II, Cat. no. 345, Fig. 420.

               Music : Handel, 'Ottone', Act II: duet, Gismonda and Matilda 'Notte cara, a te si deve'. Fade to dark.

SCENE SEVENTEEN

               REMBRANDT, *to him* GEERTGE. REMBRANDT *is painting a self-portrait, looking in a mirror.*

REMBRANDT   *(To himself)* Time to myself, in quiet.
               Concentrate,
               And try to paint your face beyond the mask,
               See through the bags and wrinkles. Peace at
               last,
               As in a wood, after a night of rain,
               The leaves and branches crackle with soft
               drops
               Like whispering grasshoppers or mice, silence
               Is never still ...

               Knock at door.

                       Who are you? Yes; come in.
               (Enter GEERTGE*)* Take off those dripping shawls.
               I'll dry them here.

GEERTGE   Some friends next door told me you needed
        help
        With a young baby; that your wife has died,
        And only students fill your house – young men.

REMBRANDT   If that is what you want, young men are here.

GEERTGE   No, it's not! I'm a widow. My late husband,
        Abraham Claesz, was a fine ship's musician:
        His trumpet raised the fishes and the fleet;
        But I'm alone – a good nurse housekeeper.

REMBRANDT   Do you know what an artist's house is like?

GEERTGE   I know bare girls have to catch cold to please
        Old men who buy the pictures. I've not seen
        It done; but I can guess ...

REMBRANDT   What?

GEERTGE   I have been
        married!

REMBRANDT   It's not quite as romantic as you think.
        The studio is full of earnest thoughts
        And students: stuffy, antiseptic; dull
        For hours on end. One pupil made a sketch
        Of all of us ...
        (Show slide no. 30, of Constantijn a Renesse: 'Pupils
        drawing a Nude in Rembrandt's Studio' (1649)
        Drawing. Darmstadt, Museum)
                Are you disappointed?

GEERTGE   No! That is not at all what I had thought.

REMBRANDT   It's wholly natural.

GEERTGE   Did your wife pose?

REMBRANDT   So many times – look! Saskia's all around!
        (Indicates the pictures on the walls)

GEERTGE
Well ... I might with my clothes on. Geertge
Dircx!
(Holds out her hand to be shaken)

REMBRANDT
This is an interview for housekeeper –
Someone who will care for and love my son:
Not for a model!

GEERTGE
It just crossed my mind.
But only clothed, as Saskia is! A widow
Can't be too careful.

REMBRANDT
For your interview
I'll paint you as you play with little Titus;
See how we three get on.
(Show slide no. 31, of Rembrandt: 'Holy Family with Angels' (1645) Bredius 570. St Petersburg, Hermitage)

GEERTGE
Please let me see?
I love it! And your baby. But it hurt
My back in that position for so long.
May I lie back, or lean on something soft?

REMBRANDT
There; use the bed: yes, with your clothes on.
Peer
Round the curtain. Hold it with your left arm
When I am painting it. Is that less painful?

GEERTGE
I love this! Will you draw this pillow's lace?

REMBRANDT
Put your right shoulder on it; modestly!
Now lie there as I look at your pink skin
To mould it on the canvas. *(Darken stage. Show slide no. 32, of Rembrandt: 'Young Woman in Bed' (1647) Bredius 110. Edinburgh, National Gallery of Scotland)*

GEERTGE
I like it here. It's fun. Have I the job?
(Stage still dark except for slides. Change slide to

*slide no. 33, Rembrandt: 'Ledikant'. (1644) etching,
Schwartz, 'Rembrandt's Etchings' Bartsch 186.)*

REMBRANDT   *(In darkness)* Do you have two left arms?

Pause on slide, then fade to black.

SCENE EIGHTEEN

MARIA *and* VONDEL.

VONDEL   Dear Tesselschade, Maria: are you free?

MARIA   Vondel, you could not be more welcome here.
I'm landscaping my garden rockery
To soothe my heartbeats after mockery.

VONDEL   Who dared?

MARIA   Predikants, Reverends, Smout and
          Trigland,
Guessing that Father Peter Plemp, who has
Brought many converts to the Church of Rome,
That gentle Jesuit, was guiding me,
They mocked, belittled, and expounded on
The Song of Songs in the most fleshly terms.

VONDEL   It was the Jesuits who brought me home
To Mother Church. Solomon's wedding-song
For his Princess of Egypt lifts to God
Mystical union of Christ with his Church,
The dance that all the music of the sky
With graceful courtesy of movement yields
In calm, unhurried motion through the stars,
Planets, far distant lights and nearer fire
Scalding the sunset waves to sink in night.
Beside this music of the elements
Robed in the stately seasons of the year
All other movement is clogged clumsiness.

MARIA   You wrote a poem for my wedding day
In which the goddess Juno tied me tight
In bonds of marriage, as I was a Siren
Distracting all the ships of Amsterdam.

VONDEL   You wrote a letter to me in my grief:
'God tests with many sorrows those he loves.'
Maria, come to Catholic Rome, your heart
At peace in sanctuary.

MARIA   When you talk
My thoughts lift back to childhood, and my
      home.

VONDEL   Blessèd Roemer's home to all the arts,
Poets and painters, singers, philosophers ...

MARIA   The shade of oak trees where I used to swim
In the canal that bordered on our garden ...

VONDEL   Jan Sweelinck playing the organ to full pews
At the Old Church, long after prayers were
      over
On Sunday evenings ...

MARIA   And on Sunday
      mornings
The young Prince leaving first on his black
      horse
While baldhead Salomon Verbeek's dancing
      toes
And fingers voiced the church tower's carillons
To music's rapturous confetti thrown
In peals across the streets of Amsterdam
To bless scrubbed worshippers all crowding
      home.

VONDEL   That world has passed. Now the Prince sides
      with Smouts
Of this world ...

MARIA   Does he?

VONDEL   He was a moderate,
And tolerant, but to raise cash for war
He seeks Counter-Remonstrant help of Trigland.
My admiration cools. His bloody wars
Gulp tax.

MARIA   My family no longer trade
In corn. My brother now rents out that home,
And warehouse with the coloured shutters
        called
'The Unicorn'.

VONDEL   That age has gone. Peter
Your brother who by day checks vats of wine,
Whale-oil, and brandy with a poking stick
To make sure all fill equally, receives –
As Secretary of our playwriting group –
The dedication of the filthiest play
You or I could possibly imagine!
So now I dedicate to you, instead,
My first play as a Roman Catholic
Called – what else, for a Roman celebration? –
Peter and Paul, great martyrs, greatest saints.

MARIA   Thank you for welcome into Mother Church.
You wrote a poem for my sister's birthday
Twenty-three years ago, and still your light
Shines on my family: not all is night.

Blackout.

SCENE NINETEEN

REMBRANDT *and* GEERTGE, *semi-naked, with sheet.*

GEERTGE   I'm chilled; and hopelessly behind with
        housework.
How is our picture now?

REMBRANDT   Come here and
          look!
          (Show slide no. 34, of Rembrandt: 'Susanna and the
          Elders' (1647) Bredius 516. Berlin – Dahlem,
          Gemäldegalerie)

GEERTGE   My foot was so cold, standing in that bath!
            You've made the man gripping my sheet look
                comic!
            But, Rembrandt, I love what you've done with
                me.
            I wish I really looked like that.

REMBRANDT   's your face!

GEERTGE   There's too much work for me to groom myself
            As I should for you. May I have some help?
            The daughter of a family I know,
            Slightly, has lost her father, and her home's
            Dissolved away. Please would you see the girl,
            And if you like her and she's suitable,
            Take her in with us as my helper?

REMBRANDT   Well;
            An extra mouth to feed ... You're asking me
            To interview her?

GEERTGE   *(Giggles)* Rembrandt, not as you
            Did me!

REMBRANDT   Geertge; you will be present, and
              decide.

          Fade.

SCENE TWENTY

REMBRANDT. VONDEL *playing the lute to him.*
Music : Dowland, 'Lachrimae Pavan'.

REMBRANDT   Thank you for playing as I paint – as David
Harped before Saul.

VONDEL   Poetry, painting, music
All flower from number, measure, balance,
        form,
God's own geometry. The greatest arts
Are those reflecting cosmic harmony.
Poetry finds our hearts through speaking
        pictures
Even as painting is dumb poetry.
These sister arts unite, my Rembrandt, in
Your paintings of my plays.

REMBRANDT   *(Finishing at easel)* Yes; it is done.
Here is my picture of your final speech
By David to crippled Mephibosheth
In your great Amsterdam success 'The
        Brothers'.
*(Show slide no. 35, of Rembrandt: 'The
Reconciliation of David and Mephibosheth' (1642)
Bredius 511. St Petersburg, Hermitage.)*

VONDEL   Magnificent, down to the halting spurs!
That play is my 'Electra'. You have made
My Jewish tale poignant and heroic.

REMBRANDT   Declaim the words Jan Lemmers speaks on
        stage
At this point: voice the picture.

VONDEL   'Cousin, stand
        up!
You have already said enough. Now dry

Your eyes, and follow me to court where I
Will always love you for your father's sake,
My dead, beloved Jonathan.'

REMBRANDT   Thank you.
But your own striking tableau, the stage picture
In the fourth act, is silent but compels.

VONDEL   The seven men spawned by Saul whom David
                hanged
High on stage gallows?

REMBRANDT   No wonder their lame
                cousin
Shivers and weeps!

VONDEL   My brother made the set
Strong enough to be safe on stage. He is
The theatre manager. He wants no slips.

REMBRANDT I'll stick to static action. Have you seen
I've written in the collar of Ruijtenburch,
As Banning Cocq sets out with all the watch,
The name of your play *'Gijsbrecht van
       Aemstel'*?

VONDEL   Ah! Thank you! How's that picture been
                received?

REMBRANDT Not well. 'Too dark.' 'Too much design.' 'Too
                many
People jumbled up.' They like the weapon
Sticking out at the viewer.

VONDEL   Some poets write
Obscurely, and on purpose to perplex
Their readers to assume the poet's wise.
I'm sad that in so many of your works
You choose to live in shadow like an owl.
You love the dark. Where greatness ought to be

In Christ, and all his angels' majesty,
You use a common sitter.

REMBRANDT   Harmony
Is hierarchy. My own counterpoint
Weaves common lives, like mine, which I know
       best.

VONDEL   Mix less with vulgar people. Get well dressed!

               Fade.

               SCENE TWENTY-ONE

               REMBRANDT. *Enter to him* GEERTGE *and* HENDRICKJE.

GEERTGE   Here is the girl, Hendrickje Stoffelsdaughter.
               Hendrickje; this is Rembrandt. (HENDRICKJE
               curtseys)

REMBRANDT   How old are you?

HENDRICKJE   Soon I'll be twenty-one: I'm twenty years
               Younger than you.

REMBRANDT   *(Startled)* Oh! Geertge 's
                    primed you, has she?
               How did you meet?

GEERTGE   When he was home on
                    shore,
               Free from sailing on ocean Men-o'-War,
               My husband used to march and play his horn
               At Bredevoort's rebuilt castle, for the Prince.

REMBRANDT   Rebuilt a hexagon, was it?

GEERTGE   For best
               Defence and sightlines on the enemy.

REMBRANDT   Let Hendrickje speak.

HENDRICKJE   My father met
Abraham there, and they became best friends –
Until both, and my elder brother, Berent,
Were blasted. Lightning struck the castle tower
That stored the gunpowder.

GEERTGE   Yes. The High
         Bailiff,
Baron van Haersolte, his family,
And forty men incinerated by
That thunderbolt: Abraham, Christoffel,
Berent – none could be identified.

REMBRANDT   Be gentle! Frederik Hendrik's Bredevoort ...
The centre for all the Achterhoek Region?
I know it's an important border fortress,
Across from Münster, where they make good
         linen
For canvasses.

GEERTGE   It was. The fort's charred rubble.

HENDRICKJE   My father's, and my brother Berent's, grave.

REMBRANDT   What of your mother?

HENDRICKJE   She's married again –
Jacob van Dorsten, widower: a sergeant
Under Count Graeff van Bronckhorst, from
         the same
Regiment of Frederik Hendrik's army
My father, and my drummer brother, served.

REMBRANDT   Married so soon?

HENDRICKJE   Well, Jacob has three children,
Five, three and one, besides a married
         daughter

Living far off. We liked him. He was coping ...

GEERTGE   Yes: Like an amputated octopus.

REMBRANDT   So you are on your own?

HENDRICKJE   Except for siblings,
Married; too busy to share time with me.

REMBRANDT   What can you do?

HENDRICKJE   My father was a hunter:
I've tracked the woods and grounds of
        Bredevoort.
I've had good schooling. On the fireside lists
You'll see my father was the senior tenant
Of our well-windowed house. My love is
        children.

REMBRANDT   Hendrickje. Could you scrub, and do the
        chores
To help our Geertge? She's not very well –
Finds looking after Titus and myself
More than her energy can take.

HENDRICKJE   I can.

GEERTGE   Rembrandt, I am not dying! But I've made
(Does this prove my potential as a wife?)
My will – Hendrickje, will you witness it? –
Leaving my Trumpeter's-widow's pension,
And all I have, except my clothing, to
Titus: saying that, when he grows up, he
Must give my portrait 'Looking from the Bed',
Together with one hundred guilders, to
Trijntje Beets, in Hoorn. *(To* HENDRICKJE*)* You
        see, he's given
Me jewels belonging to his late wife, Saskia,
Whose memory fills all his mind, although –
I'll tell you frankly – I now fill his bed.

REMBRANDT	Geertge! Do you have to be so explicit?
GEERTGE	It saves misunderstandings from the start.
HENDRICKJE	Is that why you have painted this vast scene Of Christ forgiving her who was obscene? Have you reversed your roles? *(Show slide no. 36, of Rembrandt: 'Christ and the Woman taken in Adultery' (1644) Bredius 566. London, National Gallery)*
GEERTGE	Hendrickje, dear, Two widowed adults can't adulterate.
REMBRANDT	Miss Stoffels: 'fornication' is the word; It's not adultery; no one is deceived.
HENDRICKJE	The face *is* Geertge! Rembrandt: will you paint Mine?
REMBRANDT	Stadholder Frederik Hendrik has, Out of a blue sky, just commissioned me To send two paintings: one, 'The Circumcision'; The other, same size, 'Shepherds' Adoration' ...
GEERTGE	He's been paid a huge sum: two thousand guilders!
REMBRANDT	Well, we could paint you for the Prince, now that He's in the giving mood. He likes young faces ...
HENDRICKJE	Have I the job, then?
REMBRANDT	If you can control Titus in a full tantrum, then it's yours.
HENDRICKJE	*(Curtseys)* I'll do my best to please you in my chores. *(Sound of child's tantrum)*

GEERTGE   *(To* REMBRANDT*)* Try to be nice to her, so that
              she'll stay.

*Show slide no. 37, of Rembrandt: 'Child having a
Tantrum' O. and E. Benesch 'The Drawings of
Rembrandt 1973, London and New York, Vol. II,
Cat. no. 401, Fig. 485. Berlin, Staatliche Museen,
Kupferstichkabinett. Leave on screen as houselights
slowly go up. Fade this slide into slide no. 38,
Rembrandt: 'Hendrickje' (1655) Bredius 111. Paris,
Musée de Louvre. Then slide no. 39, of Rembrandt:
'Self-Portrait' (1645?) Bredius 38. Karlsruhe,
Staatliche Kunsthalle.*

*Music : 'Elsjes stamelende klacht' (A. Jansen),
soprano; then 'Lieve Kyeren wat en deun?' (Bredero)
two sopranos. Tracks 44 and 2 of Compact Disc 'Jan
Steen, Painter and Storyteller' Camerata Trajectina,
Globe, GLO 6040, July 1996, Klaas Posthuma
Productions, Castricum, The Netherlands.*

END OF ACT ONE

Act Two

The Speelhouse. ISICIATA, SAPPHO, LESBIA *and*
PRINCE WILLIAM.
*Music : Handel, 'Rodelinda', Act II: duet,
Rodelinda and Bertarido 'Io t' abbraccio'.*

ISICIATA   Prince William! Why are you here alone,
without
Your courtier-friends?

WILLIAM   Because my father's
dying.

SAPPHO   Our dashing Stadholder Prince Frederik
Hendrik?

LESBIA   Who's pleasured us more than we've pleasured
him.

WILLIAM   His memory is failing; his health's gone.
He's over sixty. Maurits, his half-brother,
Succeeded to our power aged sixteen:
But I am twenty – restless and annoyed!
The French ambassador agrees with me
I should command an army in the field
To slaughter Spaniards. My sick father blocked
Permission: to save me, he said! He cares
More for the House of Orange than my glory!

SAPPHO   Perhaps he's right. Though he can kill, and
win,
He is a Greek god refined by French taste
(Learned from his mother, Louise). You can
judge
A man by how he makes love. Brooding Maurits
Expecting winter evenings to fall early

Gave way to Frederik Hendrik's springtime
    parties,
Refurbished palaces and paradisal
Gardens, Noordeinde in The Hague,
Honselaersdijk, Rijswijk, and recently
Splendour of Huis ten Bosch – all filled with
    paintings:
Many, of us!

LESBIA   Did Frederik Hendrik say
You should not visit us when you succeed
As our Stadholder? You blush! See this new
Portrait of me painted by dear Jan Steen
To hang above this table. *(Show slide no. 40, of*
Jan Steen: 'Girl offering Oysters' (c. 1658 – 1660)
The Hague, Royal Cabinet of Paintings
Mauritshuis)   I lean out
And sprinkle salt into my opened oyster
Whose softness, with my finger and my thumb,
Is held and shown to you. The curtained bed
Behind the chair protects while I invite.

ISICIATA   New violence has meant your father's been
Absent from oyster meals a long time now.
Johan de Witt, the fresh young regent, tries
To propose amnesty, but the hard-line
Counter-Remonstrant Calvinists like Smout
Advocate fighting in our peaceful streets!
Why, only yesterday two soldiers came
And drank too much. One dropped his
    trousers and,
Knocking over his stool, lifted her skirt
(Indicating SAPPHO*)*
In front of all! I wrestled with him while
Rembrandt, who should have helped, just
    sketched the brawl.
(Show slide no. 41, of Rembrandt: 'Tavern Scene' (c.
1633 – 4) Pen and bistre, wash. O. and E. Benesch
'The Drawings of Rembrandt' 1973, London and
New York, Vol. II, Cat. no. 394, Fig. 474)

SAPPHO   Why has he scratched my face out?

LESBIA   Have no fear.
He sketched you being seduced, and caught
   your leer.
(Show slide no. 42, of Rembrandt: 'Three Couples of
Soldiers and Women' (c. 1635) Pen and bistre. O.
and E. Benesch 'The Drawings of Rembrandt' 1973,
London and New York, Vol. I, Cat. no. 100 verso,
Fig. 118)
Although you fight him on the left hand side,
On the right you settle down to acquiesce.
Look at his smile of triumph to us! You
Concentrate more on what he has to do.

ISICIATA   Prince William, I have been immortalized
In a new painting by a man who has
Not met me, only heard through Rembrandt's
   pupils
Samuel Hoogstraeten and Fabritius,
Who teach the young man – his name's Jan
   Vermeer –
And sing the praises of our speelhouse here.
Please tell me I look nothing like her so
When he arrives – he's sent this on ahead –
I can retort, before he buys a bed,
That though grim Trigland wed his parents, he
Must not be glum like him, but sport carefree.
(Show slide no. 43, of Jan Vermeer: 'The Procuress'
(1656) Dresden, Gemäldegalerie)

WILLIAM   Is that my portrait on the left hand side?
He knows women delight me, but must learn
I prefer them like pheasants, in a brace,
A pair, a couple, two at a time!

LESBIA   We know,
And here unveil you revelling in full show
Painted by Jan Steen's teacher, Nicolaus
Knüpfer from Utrecht. *(Show slide no. 44, of*

Nicolaus Knüpfer: 'Bordello' (c. 1650) Amsterdam,
Rijksmuseum, and leave on screen until the end of
the scene) He is often here,
Learning from Rembrandt how to scratch that
     fringe
On the bed-curtains into the wet paint
With hard-point handle of his brush; as you
Scrape fingers down my back. Poor Knüpfer's
     wife
Died, and he sent their little baby to
A wet nurse, but within six weeks the frost
Gave baby back to mother in her grave.
He's left with a young son, and sells you this
As he's extravagantly penniless.

SAPPHO   Like Rembrandt, who is always buying things:
A bird of paradise, antlers, and horns,
Skins of a lion and a lioness,
Catapults, longbows, helmets, swords, two legs
(Human) dissected by Vesalius;
Paired globes that map the world, erotic art
By Raphael, Rosso, Annibale Caracci,
Giulio Bonasone. He buys back
His own work at intolerable prices
In auction with loans that he can't repay.

WILLIAM   I'll buy Nicolaus Knüpfer's Roman prince
With his two women to remind me of
My happy days and pollened nights spent here
(So angering my mother), when the States
General squat like wet pelicans
On my ambitions to revenge the murder
Of my grandfather by the Spaniards.

ISICIATA   William of Orange gave us our Dutch world
And freedom. Now his son is dying, you
Who take his name will not desert, forget
Us, humblest of your subjects? You come here
Unafraid and alone. What other Prince
In any country can do this? I found

My own trade through my parents' snobbery.
The wholesale dealer looked down on retail
With the contempt a tallow chandler sneered
On the hot butcher, who despised the poor
Barber, who preened it over the blacksmith,
And he the tallow chandler once again.
The daughter of a pipe tobacconist
Could not play with cheesemongers'
    daughters; so
I looked up to rich men beyond my sphere,
Like you, who flattered me and passed me on.
So I learned; and protect my girls, feed them,
Carry their debts for clothes and make-up,
    gems,
Manage their lives, and teach them to entice,
Cook, serve and sew. Our home economy
Is woman's image of Court policy.
So, when your father dies – who loved our home
And brought you here – protect this
    honeycomb.
(Fade, leaving slide on in the dark for a few seconds)

SCENE TWO

REMBRANDT *and* VONDEL.

VONDEL   Rembrandt, I have been asked to write some
    words
To bless your painting of our Mennonite
Preacher Anslo and his wife, who say
Though I have left your Baptist congregation
For Mother Rome, they'd like the two of us,
Who so long sat beneath his pulpit stool,
Both on their wall. Do you have it to hand?

REMBRANDT   I have. Cornelis Anslo takes no pay
For all his ministry. He's a good man.
This is my gift to him in gratitude

For many years of selflessness.
*(Show slide no. 45, of Rembrandt: 'Cornelis Anslo
and his Wife Aeltje' (1641) Bredius 409, Berlin-
Dahlem, Gemäldegalerie)*

VONDEL   I see.
Well, Aeltje's staring as Cornelis turns
Expounding Holy Writ ... She looks exhausted
As he proves yet another point ... Your light's
All wrong. The candle's out.

REMBRANDT   All light shines from
The Bible.

VONDEL   On the hands of his good wife?

REMBRANDT   Well, yes: perhaps they are a little pale –
But then, they fall beneath the source ...

VONDEL   Rembrandt:
Is that work finished?

REMBRANDT   Yes.

VONDEL   Hear what I'll write:
'Ah, Rembrandt, paint Cornelis' voice,
His outside's but our second choice:
Unseen he inspires through the ears
So Anslo's known by him who hears.'

REMBRANDT   Is that it?

VONDEL   The truth told in crafted verse.

REMBRANDT   No mention of my painting?

VONDEL   Rembrandt, you
Fail to obey the rules of Greece and Rome.
I've praised (in verse) your teacher, Pieter
            Lastman's

Painting 'Sacrifice at Lystra'. He
Was the Apelles of our time, outsoared
The classic masters of the ancient world
Because he knew and studied what they wrote.
You set yourself apart, and contradict
All laws of art: proportion, outline. Worse –
The beauty of a naked goddess, art's
Most perfect subject, you make pitiful,
Repugnant. Flabby washerwomen pose
With fat-rolled stomach-stretches, garter-marks,
All solemnly recorded by your brush.

REMBRANDT I paint what I see.

VONDEL   Not what could be! Ah!
There lies your fault! My tragedy of *Jephthah*
Springs from him trusting only to his
  conscience,
Not to the ancient wisdom of the priest
Who warned him not to kill his only child.

REMBRANDT Oh, Vondel! Catholic polemic.

VONDEL   Yet I have
Translated all of Virgil into Dutch
Prose.

REMBRANDT   Well, I'm trying to teach Titus Latin.
Your work will help us. *(Mischievously)* Isn't
  Virgil pagan?

VONDEL He sang the fall of ancient Troy, foresaw
The world-wide empire of Augustus – both
The fall of paganism, and the birth
Of a new Son of Jove who brings us peace,
The Virgin-born Apollo, turning time.
Learn from great statues!

REMBRANDT   Nature. I prefer
Dutch friends I live among.

VONDEL   No classic aim?
                  Grandeur? Ideals bring out the best in us.
                  The story in a picture is what tells.

REMBRANDT   I don't read much, except to help my son,
                  As my eyes need rest after daylight hours
                  Etching and painting. Truth, in what I see,
                  Can be found in a slaughtered ox.

VONDEL   The soul
                  Is all that matters, not the carcass!

REMBRANDT   Yes.
                  (Pause) A broken corpse for two days was God's
                        home.
                  Vondel, great poet, I am penniless,
                  Dishevelled; and neglected by the great.
                  Leave me to find, among the whores, and poor,
                  Integrity to keep my paintings pure.

                  Fade.

                           SCENE THREE

          HUYGENS, PRINCE WILLIAM *and* FREDERIK HENDRIK.

HUYGENS   Your father asks to see you.

WILLIAM   Why? How near
                  The end is he?

HUYGENS   Like a November leaf
                  Dancing the edge of winter. Dalliance
                  With petticoats of past authority
                  Is all that's left. Each comes to say goodbye:
                  The delegations from States General,
                  The States of Holland ... our own loyallest
                  Preacher from Delft (where father will be
                        buried)

Johannes Goethals who records it all –
The flow of dark clothes and the ebbing hours –
Now you.

WILLIAM What can I say?

HUYGENS You honour him:
Convince him you'll be wise in office, not
Irascible as with mother.

WILLIAM But she wants
Peace with Spain. I certainly do not!
By God I'll show them who's in charge!

HUYGENS The kite
Needs a sustaining wind to stay aloft.
You are young heir-apparent.

WILLIAM Why, the States
General gave me command of cavalry
When I was three years old! A great princess,
The elder daughter of King Charles of England,
Mary Stuart 's my wife. I'm twenty-one!

HUYGENS What am I? Fifty: losing teeth and friends.

WILLIAM You must make new – and start by humouring
me.

FREDERIK My son – is that your voice I hear?

HUYGENS Go in!
Listen to what he says. It matters. Take
Away that medicine of liquid gold.
He does not need it any more. Accept
His final blessing.

WILLIAM Eh? Father! I'm here!

FREDERIK You are the Orange hope in a dark sky,

My William. On you every eye is fixed.
Now immortality like pinpricks through
The starry shroud of next week beckons me,
Kneel down and swear you'll listen to advice.

WILLIAM

Father, I swear we'll give you a great send-off:
Twenty black horses with your coats of arms –
Orange, Nassau, Dietz, Geertruidenberg,
Breda of course, thanks to your victory,
Buren, Lingen, Leerdam, IJsselstein,
Grave, Flushing, Veere and Moeurs ...

FREDERIK

          I'm not
  dead yet!
Listen! Yes, walk behind me all alone
To win by pathos every heart and mind
Of those you'll rule, but hear while I still speak ...

WILLIAM

I only wanted you to know how proud
I am of all you've been.

FREDERIK

        My blessing, son.
And, while we are alone, let me say this:
The lifted skirt of princely adolescence
Must yield to subtleties of princely rule,
Negotiations and diplomacy
To seduce men now into loyalty,
Not the reverse.

WILLIAM

      Father, you learned that art
Of rule, you say, by sharing simple lives
Along the Breestraat.

FREDERIK

      Our strict Calvinists
Will close the speelhouses, and candle-snuff
Vapour the dark where laughter shaped our
  days.
The greatest battle you will ever have –
You must win, to avoid catastrophe –
Is with yourself.

WILLIAM   Why?

FREDERIK   Men's lives hang on
you;
Perhaps a country's. Please don't alienate
That web of loyalties that I have spun
Between the kingdoms, countries, provinces,
States, factions, hatreds, vested interests,
All the gradations of Christ's church on earth
Rat-eyed with watchful animosities.
Let them respect you as you leave behind
The downy peach of youth's soft, dawn-pale skin
Flushed red, so sweetly flavoured, and pluck out
The stone of future greatness from its cleft.

WILLIAM   Father, your orange-pip (as you see me)
Will grow strong, not waste into marmalade.
What is your dearest wish?

FREDERIK   To live to see
The Peace with Spain, at Münster, all agreed.

WILLIAM   You, of all people, now want peace with Spain!
You will break faith with France? With
Calvinists
Who long to free our South from popery?
The Netherlands is a worm cut in half,
The two parts quarrelling while still alive.
Spain must withdraw so we unite to rule
The oceans of the world.

FREDERIK   You fool! You fool!

WILLIAM   Here, drink your medicine and save your
tongue.

FREDERIK   I served the States. Your grandfather's chief skill
Was silence. Learn from him. My song is sung.

Fade.

SCENE FOUR

TRIGLAND, SMOUT *and* REMBRANDT.
*Music : 'Keuningskaarsje' (children's voices); then
'Sterrenlied' (children's voices with rumble-pot).
Tracks 41 and 42 of Compact Disc 'Jan Steen,
Painter and Storyteller' Camerata Trajectina, Globe,
GLO 6040, July 1996, Klaas Posthuma
Productions, Castricum, The Netherlands.*

TRIGLAND They ridicule my nose.

SMOUT   A strawberry
Lovingly cultivated with fruit of
The vine, that maketh glad the heart of man.

TRIGLAND You are immortalized by a pig's bladder
Stretched on a jar, with hole pricked in the
   centre
To make a rumble-pot, played with a stick
That's shafted up and down the orifice
To vibrate through bass rumbling ululation
Till the room empties.

SMOUT   Poem, no doubt; by
  Vondel.

TRIGLAND By scurrilous Vondel; yes. Your name in it
Is 'Barnyard Rooster with the Fattened Head'.

SMOUT The cockscomb! Dignity ignores the rabble;
And gratitude to editors is rare
As breast-fed fish.

TRIGLAND *and* SMOUT *enter* REMBRANDT *'s room.*

      Painter, you have been with
Archpoet Vondel.

REMBRANDT   True.

TRIGLAND   (*Silencing* SMOUT. *Charmingly*) We need your
        help.
        They say you're good with money and the law.

REMBRANDT   Survival nowadays necessitates
        Some ingenuity.

TRIGLAND   Yes, so we've heard.
        A recent saintly corpse has bequeathed us
        Of the Consistory his Spanish horse –
        A fine beast – to be sold: the proceeds thrown
        To beggars in the streets, no coin kept back.

REMBRANDT   I'll plant soft orphans of our speelhouse out
        To beg. What day?

TRIGLAND   'It is more blest to give
        Than to receive', Rembrandt.

SMOUT   'Give to him
        Who asks', and we would ask your good advice.
        Such a sum could do more good for the poor
        Invested in the Consistory funds.

REMBRANDT   Had he a cat?

SMOUT   A cat?

REMBRANDT   Yes. Did he leave
        A goat, a hen, a pig?

TRIGLAND   He left a goose.

REMBRANDT   Then take them both, sell at the market fair
        In one lot, jointly: one guilder for the horse
        One hundred for the goose.

TRIGLAND   Whoever buys
        Gains a great stallion for a decent sum
        One hundred and one guilders, goose thrown in.

SMOUT   *(Thinking)* But as the horse was only priced at
                     one
                 Guilder, that is all we give away!
                 We are most grateful to you.

REMBRANDT   But you say
                 You look for Vondel?

TRIGLAND   All who celebrate
                 The speelhouses, *(Sadly)* as you do, and your
                     friends.

REMBRANDT   Augustine, that great doctor of the church,
                 Writes 'No man sins in what he can't avoid.'

SMOUT   The body is the tabernacle of
                 The Holy Spirit. It must be well flogged
                 Into submission.

TRIGLAND   Martin Luther says
                 Women who sell love are abomination;
                 Corrupting and enticing young men. One
                 Syphilitic, stinking, scabby whore
                 Can poison ten – a hundred – decent sons
                 Of godly parents. She should be condemned
                 As murderer, worse than a poisoner.

SMOUT   Tools of the Devil sent to bewitch students!
                 Look at the University of Paris! It's
                 The Pope's whoring chamber! Human
                     reason –
                 The Devil's harlot – replaces works of faith.

REMBRANDT   For those who have no money, speelhouses
                 Are courteous eating places where the afraid,
                 The lonely, and the unloved can make new
                     friends
                 Gently, at little cost. No one need 'sin'.
                 Whatever age, whatever state you are,
                 There, poetry and music can be shared.

SMOUT   Speelhouse – the poor man's university!

REMBRANDT   And women's.

SMOUT   What a grotesque blasphemy!
                   Upheld by fornication?

REMBRANDT   That's not sin.

TRIGLAND   (*Interested*) What do you mean?

REMBRANDT   Abraham's wife,
                      Sarai,
                   Infertile, begged him make love to her maid,
                   Hagar. Was this fornication sin?
                   Rachel guided Jacob, her own husband,
                   To penetrate her maid Bilhah, while she
                      clasped
                   The girl between her knees. Was fornication
                   Here a sin? No; blessing! When Leah became
                   Infertile, she smiled Zilpah, her handmaid,
                   To do the same. Their sons are 'Genesis'.
                   Sin is the opposite of charity.
                   Love of our neighbour may hurt no one, no,
                   Not even God.

TRIGLAND   You misuse Scripture.

REMBRANDT   How?
                   Joshua's men lay in the house of Rahab
                   The harlot. She's praised by St. James. And look:
                   Women when angry can be dangerous
                   To men like you who enter when not wanted.
                   Sisera came to Jael in her tent.
                   He asked for water and she gave him milk.
                   She brought him butter in a lordly dish,
                   Covered him with her rug, and when he lay
                   Exhausted, sleeping, hammered a tent peg
                   Right through his skull into the ground, in spite
                   Of body-squirming. Here's my version.

(Show slide no. 46, of Rembrandt: 'Jael and Sisera'
(c. 1648 – 9) Pen and bistre. O. and E. Benesch
'The Drawings of Rembrandt' 1973, London and
New York, Vol. III, Cat. 622a, Fig . 797)

SMOUT   Ugh!
I think it's time we left. Remember, sin
Is grievous in proportion as it pleases.
St. Paul writes: 'Sensuous pleasure is most
          fierce';
So fornication is the gravest sin.

REMBRANDT   Our Lord even forgave adultery,
And said: 'Neither do I condemn thee ...'
(Show slide no. 47, of Rembrandt: 'Christ and the
Woman taken in Adultery' (1644) Bredius 566.
London, National Gallery)
                                        Mercy
Is all.

TRIGLAND   It subverts law. As Calvin says:
'No man should read Holy Scripture alone,
Just for himself.' He calls our Reformed
          Church
'God's faithful watchwoman' who guards to see
That God's truth never disappears.

REMBRANDT   Music
Breathing the window of a bride at dawn
Waking her day, dissolves such moral glue,
Forgives, forgets slips made since she was born:
The fawn of joy leaps through the morning
          dew.

Fade.

SCENE FIVE

FABRITIUS *and* HOOGSTRAETEN.

HOOGSTRAETEN Why did she die?

FABRITIUS   My wife? Lost dream? My
                 Aeltge?
            She lived next door. We'd peep, knock on the
                 wall;
            Married when I was nineteen. Then we came
            Here, so that I could learn from Rembrandt. In
            Less than eighteen months scurvy had plucked
            Out grace and happiness, root, leaf and flower.

HOOGSTRAETEN My first engraving was of scurvy-grass
            For Doctor Beverwijk's book on the foul
            Disease. The medicine stilled from this cress
            I thought cured scurvy! That's what the book
                 said;
            That's why I etched it.

FABRITIUS   Well, her gums swelled up,
            Spots like plum-tinted dandelions spread
            Over the whiteness of her softest skin.
            I tried to paint her. Rembrandt finished it
            For me after she died, as I'd lost heart.
            *(Show slide no. 48, of Rembrandt: 'Young Woman at
            an Open Door' (1645) Bredius 367. Chicago, Art
            Institute)*
            No more of this. My pupil, Jan Vermeer,
            Is coming to be introduced to Rembrandt.

HOOGSTRAETEN I liked his painting of our speelhouse friends
            As he imagines them.

FABRITIUS   The boy has gifts
            That could out-paint us all.

HOOGSTRAETEN   When I came here
                    Sometimes I'd go without all food or drink
                    Crying into my paints as I worked on
                    Until I'd mastered the fault Rembrandt had
                    Just rubbed my nose in.

FABRITIUS   He is gentler, now.

Enter VERMEER.

                    Jan Vermeer! Welcome!

VERMEER   Carel Fabritius,
                    Thank you for teaching me. Did my large
                        canvas
                    Of your procuress come to you in time
                    For William, Prince of Orange, to enjoy?

FABRITIUS   Yes, it arrived. He saw it: didn't buy.
                    At least he knows your style, and interests.

VERMEER   I've painted two more with your speelhouse
                        girls
                    In, copied from Dirck van Baburen's
                    Great picture 'The Procuress'. Actually,
                    I've reproduced, on the back wall of each,
                    His entire painting: in one to reflect,
                    Mirror my group of three; *(Show slide no. 49, of*
                    Vermeer: 'The Concert' (n.d.) Boston, Isabella
                    Stewart Gardner Museum) the other shows
                    A young girl, 'cello unstroked, what's in store
                    As she plays virginals beneath the whore.
                    (Show slide no. 50, of Vermeer: 'Young Woman seated
                    at Virginals' (n.d.) London, National Gallery)

                    Enter REMBRANDT.

REMBRANDT   Whose work is this? Some son of Baburen?

HOOGSTRAETEN   Jan Vermeer. You saw his speelhouse painting

Sent on ahead. Here are two more: all dreams.

REMBRANDT   I like the composition, and the colours,
But cut your apron-strings to Baburen –
Don't quote him in each picture! It is clear
You've never sampled mercenary love.

VERMEER   Please take me to your speelhouse! Here is one
As I imagine these two *(Indicating* FABRITIUS *and*
HOOGSTRAETEN*)*   choosing me
A lady, as they've promised.
*(Show slide no. 51, of Vermeer: 'Girl being offered
Wine' (n.d.) Brunswick, Herzog Anton Ulrich-
Museum)*

REMBRANDT   I must laugh!

VERMEER   Now let me make you cry. You have a gift
From me.

REMBRANDT   A gift? Is it another painting?
No, you must sell them, not give all away!
That's what I tell my pupils. Price them well
So rich men talk about them till they sell.

VERMEER   No. It's the death-mask of Prince Frederik
Hendrik. *(Gives mask to* REMBRANDT*)*

HOOGSTRAETEN Good God!

FABRITIUS   *(Angrily)* You should have asked me
first!

REMBRANDT   *(Holding and looking at the death mask)* This Prince
Will stay with me until I die. You see,
He bought my paintings and was kind to me:
So shall I be to you. *(Music : Handel, 'Ottone',
Act II: duet, Gismonda and Matilda 'Notte cara, a
te si deve')*   The speelhouse din!
Come, celebrate! And break this young man in!

SCENE SIX

The Speelhouse.

The characters from the previous scene meet ISICIATA, LESBIA *and* SAPPHO. *To them, later,* LIEVENS, TRIGLAND *and* SMOUT.

ISICIATA   Rembrandt and pupils – are you ready now
To see unveiled the portrait Willem Drost
Has paletted to hang by Lesbia's bed
Looking down on it as she earns her keep?
You've taught him well. Most sensuous of your
     students,
Drost's made enticement irresistible.

REMBRANDT   Come! Show us all before the pancakes burn.
(Show slide no. 52, of Willem Drost: 'Bathsheba'
(1654) Paris, Louvre)
So that's what Drost's been fondling with his
     brush!
On her chemise he's phased the white to grey
Gradations till her skin glows from the dark
Through tones and shadows of her smooth-
     touched warmth
To focus eyes on one, sole, centred nipple
Palpable as her heavy, offered breast.

LESBIA   But is it like me? That tilt gave me neck-ache.
The jewels look good. The necklace wasn't
     much.

FABRITIUS   Your head takes second place in that spotlight.
What are you cherishing in your left hand?

SAPPHO   A napkin to sneeze into. Lesbia,
Our world depends on fantasies, and dreams,
What might be, when we lock the door alone
With secret time to let our thoughts run riot.

Here, we interpret what men are afraid
To say, but long for. If your hair's unwashed,
Your bust sags, anchovies hang on your breath,
He'll look up, while you're riding, past your ear
And see Drost's version of what you could be.

HOOGSTRAETEN   Let me remind you, ladies, we've a guest –
Jan Vermeer from Delft, studying with us.
Isiciata; Sappho; Lesbia;
He's painted his own fantasy of you
To sell to the new Prince of Orange, but
William has not yet purchased Vermeer's bait.

VERMEER   Not for one moment did I dream you were
So beautiful, amusing, welcoming!
The Predikants paint sermon-horrors of
Dishonest, godless, rowdy, diseased pits
Where fighting and disruption bring the watch
(And shame) to unwashed, drunken clients,
    robbed
And beaten, cheated, damned in health and
    soul:
Yet what I see and hear is self-control;
Shared laughter; comfort and protection, joy
Grown from goodwill that sorrow can't destroy.
No wonder painters pay to see your glow
And create masterpieces. Poetry
Blushes with song to feel your harmony
Of women's friendship, in a world of men,
That still finds room for tenderness, and then
Fulfils and satisfies without regret
Honest agreement with blonde or brunette,
So that sweet memory makes each return
To this community, where we unlearn
The heartache and defeats, betrayals, pain
Of the harsh world; here, learn to love again.

HOOGSTRAETEN   Vermeer, your paintings show your peace of
    mind
And gentle innocence. Perhaps you're right.

Financial trust is joy's foundation – but
Fights, and unwelcome visitors do come.
Isiciata rules, enforces calm
And churchgoing, and doctors' careful balm.
We men are visitors and have no say
In how she runs her safe, well-ordered day.

ISICIATA   Well! What a compliment! Jan Vermeer, in
This city, with so many men abroad
In the East Indies, on the seas, at war
In battlefields away from home, there are
Three adult Christian women to two men.
Think what this means. The speelhouse is a
          home
To many girls who'd starve; die young. All I
Regret is this has made me infertile. That
Upsets me when I think about it. Tell
Me I act mother to my girls?

FABRITIUS   Too well!
Why, you know all our secrets! Help us now.
Vermeer has never seen a speelhouse, though
His mind and fancies think of little else.
As the proud wind shrugs down the new-born
          foal
Trying to stand, unsteady, shivering,
Until the mare's flank shields to try again, ,
So help our student to become a man.

LESBIA   (*To* VERMEER) You've seen my secrets spread
          before you in
Drost's tantalizing mirror of my charms.
I teach the ladybird to spread each wing,
The sun to climb back up the sky for spring,
Night to run backwards while my loving
          arms
Play all the harmonies of rustling sheets
While rhythms of the heart beat as we cling.

REMBRANDT   Sappho, can you outbid her gorgeous treats?

SAPPHO   Stop the round world! Now! Distant countries,
                             hush!
                     Nature has given me a painter's brush
                     Quite beyond Rembrandt's. It creates delight,
                     Can turn a great whale belly up to sight
                     For tickling, while the glancing moon delays,
                     To peer, and join in love that holidays
                     With such abandoned, passioned ecstasy
                     That bridegrooms-for-a-night ignite with me.

VERMEER   May I have both?

                     Enter LIEVENS.

LIEVENS   Charcoal, old friend: I'm back
                     From years of travel with a gift for you
                     Of our fun here. Why, even the same girls!
                     (Kisses them)

SAPPHO   Jan Lievens home, blowing hot coals again!
                     Well, what a night ahead! Here's Jan Vermeer
                     On his first visit to us. Please stand on
                     The table, high – there! Now we all can see!

VERMEER   Why? Here I feel exposed! Your present, sir,
                     For Rembrandt. Come. I'll hold for all to view.
                     (Show slide no. 53, of Jan Lievens: 'Mars and Venus'
                     (1653) Berlin, Staatliche Schlösser und Gärten)

LESBIA   The Prince of Orange with our Sappho on
                     Her best professional form! A child reveals
                     The opposite of what the Prince conceals.

                     TRIGLAND *and* SMOUT *burst open the door.*

SMOUT   All carnal intercourse cease where you are!
                     The magistrates and the Consistory
                     Close all the speelhouses. Here's the decree!
                     Notorious sin, it is thought good that, now,
                     In open presence of you all, God's curse,

Out of the Book of Deuteronomy
In chapter twenty-seven, be pronounced
To the intent that, being admonished by
God's indignation against mortal sin
You flee from vices, and affirm this curse
From God with your own mouths, and say:
    'Amen'.
'Cursèd be he that fornicates and lies
Beside and in his neighbour's wife. Amen.'
(No one joins in save TRIGLAND*)*

ISICIATA   May paint-wet fangs of ships' prows sink into
Your twin-globed rumble-pot, dangle you out
Above ten half-starved sharks, who each confer
Which part of you will be their gum-stick. Out!
I'll beat you with this broom until the fat
Leaks down in sweat and slims you court-card
    flat!
(Beats him)

TRIGLAND   *(Reading)* From Holy Sacraments, and
    absolution,
From the community of Christ on earth,
And from all benefactions, and divine
Blessings and spiritual healings, you
Are blasted and excluded from this day
By proclamation of Consistory
Of the Reformed Dutch Church of
    Amsterdam!

LIEVENS   *(To* VERMEER, *who is still holding up the picture –
slide is still showing)*
Vermeer, let's beat both – goat, and bleating
    ram!

Uproar. Fade.

SCENE SEVEN

MARIA *(one-eyed). To her* HUYGENS *and* PRINCE
WILLIAM.

MARIA

Sir Constantijn! Our Prince! You grace my
    home
And honour me who ought to honour you.

WILLIAM

Huygens was teaching me your father's verse.
Are these the words he sang when you were
    young?
        'Riches, mother of much evil,
           Wife of treachery,
        Sister of hatred and upheaval,
           Daughter of jealousy,
        When you're ours we live in fear,
        But your lack brings sorrow's tear.'

MARIA

You are so accurate you conjure up
Memories of Muiden Castle long ago –
Head-poet Hooft its sheriff, Barlaeus
My wooer, Vossius – Greek scholar, Laurens
Reael, Governor of our East Indies,
Reading his titillating verse of love –
Above all, you – Constantijn Huygens, with
Your love of English poetry and John
    Donne,
Whom you heard preach, and was among your
    friends,
But Vondel mocked for his obscurity.

HUYGENS

Ah Vondel!
           'Britain's Donne
           Is a dark sun.
      If dearest Tesselschade
          Peers through the smoke
          To see his joke
      She'll have to peep much harder.'

WILLIAM He wrote that! Catholic Vondel scorns the
        songster.

MARIA   John Donne was Catholic throughout his youth.

HUYGENS But in maturity Dean of St. Paul's
        Cathedral. You have sailed the other way
        And lost an eye (but how?) observing Rome.

MARIA   A blacksmith beating out my horse's shoe
        Sparked an iron sliver stinging me half dark.

HUYGENS Your ruined face, now blacksmith-shattered,
        Bows before idols Zwingli scattered.

MARIA   You voyage with silly people: Trigland, Smout.
          Come home to Mother Church!
        Don't navigate by guess work. Be devout,
          Rome's compass guide your search.

WILLIAM You two have much in common: skill with wit,
        Verse, languages. I hunt in Gelderland
        When not in politics with Mazarin
        And D'Estrades; preserving Calvin's milk,
        Curdled in Spanish Netherlands; deposing
        Those new-born Oldenbarnevelts the Bicker
        Brothers, Andries and Cornelis. Well,
        At least they've kept their heads!

MARIA   What's your
        decree?

WILLIAM That they resign from city government,
        Withdraw for ever from all public life.

HUYGENS Neatly combining mercy with success!

WILLIAM Will you hunt with us, Tesselschade?

MARIA   *(Declining)* Prince,

You sweat. Have you a fever? Music may
Calm the high temperatures of State away.

WILLIAM   I'm grateful; but all wait – the horses, hounds,
And leaf-ripped, harsh October blows around
My raw-hot cheeks to cool me. Gracious friend,
Thank you for welcome. Proudest stags must
      bend.
(They bow and depart)

Fade on MARIA.

SCENE EIGHT

REMBRANDT *and* HENDRICKJE.

REMBRANDT   Yes, stand my love – half-way up to your knees.

HENDRICKJE   Doesn't it look a little odd to have
An inside scene with oriental drapes
Heavy with red and gold, me in my nightshirt,
With my feet standing in a running stream?

REMBRANDT   It's not a stream.

HENDRICKJE   Well, love, it looks like it!

REMBRANDT   Wait till I've finished. Could you loop your lap
So that it covers your hairs? Yes; look down –
      good! –
At your reflection as you take it off.
I want to catch that moment in a sketch
In oils, with bold, fine brush-strokes, quickly
      drawn.
Here, let me show you how to lift that linen
Into a smile's shape. (REMBRANDT *goes to
rearrange her nightdress*)

Enter GEERTGE.

GEERTGE   Caught you both at it!
                    This is what's stopped me sleeping in your bed!
                    Hendrickje Stoffels: I'll empty your chamber-
                         pot
                    Over your head.

HENDRICKJE   Have you got widow's twitch?
                    Loose-teethed insanity with sudden rages?

GEERTGE   I saw him use his hand on you! Just look!
                    About to share a bath together? Paint
                    Is just a cover for your passion's heat.

REMBRANDT   Geertge! You came to me when I was white
                    With anguish, and you've given all your help.
                    You asked me to accept Hendrickje, for
                    Your sake. Her body is my inspiration now.

GEERTGE   As mine has been ... It's just that I am ill!

REMBRANDT   And I need loving; and she gives it me.

GEERTGE   Well, chase the dappled shadows round her
                         knees,
                    And play with her while her two blue feet freeze.
                    I know what it is like, Hendrickje. I
                    Posed as Susanna with one foot all wet
                    For hours, with backache. Oh, you may be young
                    And think you've found a father who's named
                         'Lot' –
                    Whose daughters made him drunk, to breed
                         from him,
                    (Yes, he has painted it) – but I will beat
                    You with a ladle till that bottom's raw,
                    Lift up that rag and show you've played the
                         whore
                    To all the world! Gouda's Correction House
                    Will castigate you, if the Spinhouse won't.
                    The easy days are passing. Calvinists
                    Peer into every corner where you've pissed.

HENDRICKJE   Geertge, I care for you. I'm grateful for
All you arranged to bring me here. It seems
Ungrateful of me to love and be loved
By Rembrandt; but he has not married you.
He is a free man; you are a free woman.
If what you say were true, and Rembrandt's hand
Was holding me, he needs to understand
The little kicks down there are his own child.

GEERTGE   *(Realizing that she has lost)* Snake-riding Eve! No
         wonder I'm reviled.
I trusted your false innocence you've used,
Ruthlessly, to usurp my man from me ...

REMBRANDT   Geertge, get out! I mean it. You're insane.
I do not want to see you here again.

GEERTGE   That's all the thanks I have for seven years
Devoted to your service. Well: I'm gone!
What might have been's just a forgotten song.
(Exit GEERTGE*)*
*(Show slide no. 54, of Rembrandt: 'Hendrickje
Bathing' (1655) Bredius 437. London, National
Gallery, on otherwise dark stage)*

SCENE NINE

REMBRANDT *and* HENDRICKJE *at Bredevoort.*

HENDRICKJE   Darling, it's good you have left Amsterdam
A little while to see my Bredevoort.

REMBRANDT   I'm glad Ten Vliete-Swart and Lijsbeth asked
You to be God-mother to their Geertruijtt;
That I'm invited, too.

HENDRICKJE   I think they like you.
My families accept you now. Oh darling,
I love to show you all my childhood haunts

Round Bredevoort – our brick and oak-
          beamed homes
In friendly, narrow streets around the church
And square, where the pump gushes. You saw
          how
This sleepy centre of a busy town's
Woken by children hooping here from school
To burn up energy; or, as I did,
Find out the fields, and leave the busy drone
Of daily adult worries driving wheels
To stomach-lie with chin on ground among
Long, seeding grasses where small insects play
Clinging, like mud to a slipped bottom's dress;
Hiding, when home's anxiety calls out
Across the darkening meadows, the owls'
          polder,
With canal-bittern's booming breeding-call
And church bell tolling Evensong and food.

REMBRANDT   Thank you for bringing me. I love it here –
          All the ideas it gives me: and what trees!

HENDRICKJE   Woods, fields – all part of a huge force of nature
          Driving new life, and rounding out in me.
          I wish you could have met my father! He
          Loved little children; would have kissed our
                    babe.
          Feel her?

REMBRANDT   A girl?

HENDRICKJE   You have a boy.

REMBRANDT   Dear Titus.
          A sister for him?

HENDRICKJE   Yes. Air on my cheeks
          Changes from sun to soft with evening's star.
          We must go back. They'll wonder where we are.

          Exeunt.

SCENE TEN

VERMEER. VONDEL *to him.*

VONDEL   Ah! Young Vermeer! Huffing through the cold
To the bleak auction of all Rembrandt's goods?
*(*VERMEER *nods)* We'll walk together. These are
      bitter days.
Prince William's died – we thought while
      hunting: some
Say it was smallpox. Just three years he held
The post of stadholder; tried to enlarge
Its power, to fight Spain.

VERMEER   He was twenty-four.
One year younger than I am. Tesselschade –
Maria, Roemer's daughter, bluestocking
Poet, has gone.

VONDEL   Her last remaining daughter's
Death, aged nineteen, stole from her all will
To live. She was unique among her sex.
Eusebia, I called her in my praise
That dedicates to her one of my plays:
Peter and Paul. She had lost all she loved;
Yet still was brave, wise, deeply gentle, kind,
Intelligent above all womankind.
When I think how the blind Consistory
Has treated Rembrandt's woman Hendrickje
With excommunication for whoredom
And fornication, Vermeer, I despair
At death of charity.

VERMEER   What can you say
About the election of Johan de Witt
To be the new Councillor Pensionary?
Is he a statesman who consolidates,
Blends colours of this country's palette,
      while

The newest Prince of Orange is a baby
Posthumously born?

VONDEL   Johan de Witt
Is skilled in politics, a honey tongue,
A resurrected Oldenbarnevelt.
The House of Orange will pale into gold.
Disclose your painting.

VERMEER   I'm a little shy,
Showing a seventy-year-old public man,
A mighty poet, my poor daubings ...

VONDEL   Cease!
What is it?

VERMEER   A geographer.

(Show slide no. 55, of Vermeer: 'The Geographer'
(1669) Frankfurt, Städelsches Kunstinstitute)

VONDEL   You've caught
The moment that he stops his work. The light
Makes every object clear and solid. Reason
Dominates, unlike Rembrandt's etching 'Faust'
(Show slide no. 56, of Rembrandt: 'Faust' (c. 1652)
Etching, dry point and engraving; Schwartz,
'Rembrandt's Etchings', 1977. Bartsch 270)
Which I own, where the supernatural
Bursts in to interrupt Faust, make him rise
From his desk to confront bright mystery
In a dark world. His globe is scarcely
            sketched.
Yours, heavy, prosaic, natural-daylight-lit
By the plain window, 's tone-deaf to the spirit.
Well! We can't all, say Calvinists, find God;
Only the saved. What nonsense! Do you know
Thuringian Bloodfriends now pool all their
            wives
As means of grace to be of the elect?

VERMEER   For them body is not at war with soul
           But spiritualized pathway to the divine –
           Grace through delight! I miss the speelhouse.

VONDEL   Come.
           Rembrandt's lost all he owns, for Christmas. He
           Will need emotional support from me.
           What will you bid for? ... *(Exeunt)*

SCENE ELEVEN

REMBRANDT *and* HENDRICKJE. *Cradle on floor.*

REMBRANDT   Is it exhaustion runs tears down your cheeks?

HENDRICKJE   Probably, darling. Is our baby looking
             Up at you?

REMBRANDT   No, sound asleep – and breathing!

HENDRICKJE   I can't forget that stuffy afternoon
             When I stood in the Church's Council Room
             While old men – far from pregnant! – sat,
                     charged me
             With 'fornication': said I could no more
             Come to our Lord's Supper.

REMBRANDT   You were brave.
             Never have I admired you more than then.
             They were impressed, themselves: lifted your
                     ban
             So our Cornelia, bless her, could be christened.
             How can I cheer and please you?

HENDRICKJE   Rembrandt,
                 darling:
             Talk to me as you've never talked before;
             While I am resting.

REMBRANDT   Yes, of course I will!

HENDRICKJE   However hard my question?

REMBRANDT   Yes. My aim
                Is to reach out beyond the surface skin
                And paint you as you are – your inner life:
                Thinking, feeling – complex thoughts and
                    moods –
                To probe and understand and show the world
                The deepest workings of my loved one's mind.

HENDRICKJE   *(Playfully)* So you would sell, through all your
                    pupils' copies,
                Your wife's unguarded secret modesty?
                That's what I want to know: Geertge told me
                Everything she did was dwarfed, undermined
                By your ideal, your memory of Saskia.

REMBRANDT   There was some truth in that: but not with you.

HENDRICKJE   But so this does not happen, I must know
                What drove you, bound you both so, sexually.
                Will you tell me your shared and private
                    games
                So I can take them up, fulfil your dreams?
                And do what she did, for your sake; and more.
                What were the secrets gluing you together?

REMBRANDT   Will you be gentle with the memories
                If – and it's hard – I tell you private thoughts
                And fantasies? We are most vulnerable
                When trusting at so deep a level.

HENDRICKJE   Yes,
                My dearest love. Just share now, unabashed
                Unafraid; use whatever words you like.
                I feel so close to you. (Cornelia sleeping?

REMBRANDT   Soundly. One arm's out.

HENDRICKJE   No harm.) It's not
I want to exorcise her memory,
Only fulfil it.

REMBRANDT   I am not the same
As when I lived with her: more introspective
Now – I have a different depth of feeling
For you: affection, love, respect. You bring
Powerful physical attractiveness
And depth of insight into how I spark.
You are my mirror into which I peer
For each self-portrait – half reflecting you,
And half my Titus: both of you, myself.
All God's.

HENDRICKJE   But Saskia was not condemned.

REMBRANDT   No; nor are you. She loved the atmosphere
Of the old Speelhouse – where you'd never go,
But she would, often. As my pictures sold
So well of her, she felt she was being bought
For her attractiveness, just like a whore
Without the customary act or guilt.
This so excited her that she would be
My courtesan.

HENDRICKJE   Then let that whore be me.
*(Show slide no. 57, of Rembrandt: 'Hendrickje at an
Open Door' (1656) Bredius 116. Berlin-Dahlem,
Gemäldegalerie)*
Paint me as you did her, Rome's brothel
      goddess
Flora, bedecked with Nature, offering flowers.
*(Show slide no. 58, of Rembrandt: 'Hendrickje as
Flora' (1654) Bredius 114. New York, Metropolitan
Museum of Art)*
Think of me married to Uriah; you –
King David – sending me a letter that
Seduces me, Bathsheba, to your bed;
Although I'm torn with conscience, acquiesce:

Since you have seen me naked, and are King,
I give in to your power as your plaything.

REMBRANDT   Generous as always! If I paint you now,
The thoughtful sadness, and resigned regret
Tempered with love and womanly desire
Will make a nude that all men will admire.

HENDRICKJE   You may. And – dare I ask – something for me?
Repaint her early Venus, with my face?

REMBRANDT   Your body, too! I'll change the sheen, the
        hand's
Old gesture to your own; mature the beauty
Into a warmth and fullness that will catch
Bathsheba's poignance in a perfect match.
(Show slide no. 59, of Rembrandt: 'Danae'
(1636/56) Bredius 474. St Petersburg, Hermitage)

HENDRICKJE   Although I'm now forbidden to love Christ
In his own bread and wine, I know He cares;
And through our love may meet Him
        unawares.

Fade to a dark stage.
Show slide no. 60, of Rembrandt: 'Christ and the
Woman of Samaria' (1659) Bredius 592A. St
Petersburg, Hermitage. Pause. Then fade into slide
no. 61, Rembrandt: 'Bathsheba with King David's
Letter' (1654) Bredius 521. Paris, Musée du Louvre.

SCENE TWELVE

TITUS *and* REMBRANDT.

TITUS   I do not want to do this homework!

REMBRANDT   Learn
Your Latin.

TITUS   School should be abolished. How
                    Does one retire?

REMBRANDT   You don't.

TITUS   At fourteen?

REMBRANDT   No.
                    That sort of thing is only for the rich
                    We're stripped of everything.

TITUS   Father, we're not.
                    Mother's legacy is ours!

REMBRANDT   Look, half of that,
                    Titus, was mine. It's gone. The other half,
                    Which I may borrow till you come of age
                    Or marry, is – yes – yours: so you own me,
                    And you should pay me pocket-money.

TITUS   Well,
                    If you will let me stop this Virgil prep ...

REMBRANDT   You must know Virgil to be civilized!

TITUS   No one would call you that. You read me some
                    Stories from Ovid. Ovid's much more fun ...

REMBRANDT   Look! Stick that crimson cap around your head,
                    Sit at your desk as though you did some work,
                    Draw, if you like – I'll give you a good theme –
                    And just be quiet while I paint you.

TITUS   What,
                    Again?

REMBRANDT   Quiet! *(He paints)* Meleager was a prince,
                    Son of the King of Calydon. He loved
                    To hunt. A boar was ravaging the land,
                    Trampling young corn and rooting up the vines,

Tusking the cattle with hot, foam-flecked grunts
And blood-red eyes. His nail-sharp prickles
        tossed
For crushing all dogs who attacked. Our prince
Called out for volunteers to hunt this boar.
One was a woman with a boyish face,
An ivory quiver and a buckled robe
Clasped from her neck. Loving this Atalanta,
He flung his spear. It grounded. The boar
        charged.
His second spear shatters its shoulder-blade
Spirting the boar's blood as it whirls and crashes
Round and round, its red stream warm and
        hissing
Till all that massive energy lies still.
Meleager strips the bristling skin,
The hedgehog head with elephantine tusks,
And places them in Atalanta's lap
To thrill her. This caused jealousy ...

TITUS   It's done!
        Please look.
        (Show slide no. 62, of Titus van Rijn: 'Meleager and
        Atalanta', drawing, pen and brown wash. London,
        Clifford Duits Collection)

REMBRANDT   The dogs are good. You've given him arrows!
                And
        The boar's head is not clear; but still – well done!
        Here is my glimpse of you.
        (Show slide no. 63, of Rembrandt: 'Titus at his Desk'
        (1655) Bredius 120. Rotterdam, Museum Boymans-
        van Beuningen)

        Enter HENDRICKJE.

HENDRICKJE   Beautiful, darling!
        Stop your homework, Titus, now. It's time ...

TITUS   Why are we selling all our toys, Hendrickje?

REMBRANDT   You know why. Creditors shark up our loans,
Liquidate precious memories, gouge out
All stomach of our hopes. See this self-portrait ...
*(Show slide no. 64, of Rembrandt: 'The Anatomy
Lecture of Dr Jan Deyman' (1656) Bredius 414.
Amsterdam, Rijksmuseum)*

HENDRICKJE   (What do you mean – 'self-portrait'?

REMBRANDT   How I feel.)
Commissioned for the surgeons' guild, thanks to
My good friend Jan Six, generous poet, who
Lent me, interest-free, one thousand guilders.
Well, that bad loan he passed on to the richest,
Cruellest sneer in Amsterdam, who claims –
With interest, now: the grasping Gerbrand
     Ornia.

HENDRICKJE   I've thought about your idea. We will form
A company, your son and I, to sell
Your work. Give everything to us. We shall
Employ you with no salary: just board
And lodging.

REMBRANDT   I've transferred the deeds, to Titus,
Of this house.

HENDRICKJE   Then you have a little shield
Against the storm and hail of creditors.
Each work we sell earns for the company;
So we'll nest out a refuge where you can
Create in untormented peace.

REMBRANDT   My love,
You spend your health in saving us. How can
I thank you?

HENDRICKJE   Paint us; and have copies made:
Titus reading; *(Show slide no. 65, of Rembrandt:
'Titus Reading' (1656) Bredius 122. Vienna,*

Kunsthistorisches Museum) or dressed as a monk.
*(Show slide no. 66, of Rembrandt: 'Titus in Monk's
Habit' (c. 1660) Bredius 306. Amsterdam,
Rijksmuseum)*

REMBRANDT   I shall. I'll paint you as in happier days,
As lovely as Drost's 'Lesbia' ...

HENDRICKJE   Cover me,
If I'm to be compared to her. Some days
I do not like my body as it is.

TITUS   You still look fairly healthy.

REMBRANDT   Here's my thanks:
A father's blessing. *(Show slide no. 67, of
Rembrandt: 'Jacob Blessing the Sons of Joseph'
(1656) Bredius 525. Kassel, Gemäldegalerie)* Now;
let's pay the banks!

SCENE THIRTEEN

Auction Room: Keizerskroon Inn.

THOMAS HARINGH, TITUS *and* REMBRANDT.

TITUS   Be gentle with my father. He has dreaded
Today for eighteen months.

HARINGH   Titus, I will.

REMBRANDT   Thomas Haringh, Warden of our Town Hall.

HARINGH   Bailiff, today, of the Insolvency
Court. You've been to many of my auctions:
I never thought I should preside at yours.

TITUS   *(Indicating audience)* What a huge crowd!

HARINGH   Let's
            hope they bid up high
            And clear some of your debts.

REMBRANDT   What may I keep?

HARINGH   Your needs, to earn your living as an artist ...

TITUS   Why, that is all of this!

HARINGH   Minimum needs –
            Day-to-day clothes; the big oak chest for linen,
            Studio partitions for your pupils; just
            Necessities. Two stoves.

REMBRANDT   I know. I'll leave
            Rather than listen to the dealers' comments.
            Here is a buyer with long donkey's-ears.
            (Show slide no. 68, of Rembrandt: 'The Asinine Art-
            buyer' (1644) Pen and bistre. Benesch A35a. New
            York, Metropolitan Museum of Art)
            Excuse my bottom-wiping on the right.

HARINGH   Dear Rembrandt; I'll do all I can for you.

            TITUS *and* REMBRANDT *exeunt.*

            (To audience. Bangs gavel) Today we sell in three
                  lots, starting with
            The personal possessions, listed here,
            Belonging to Rembrandt van Rijn, the artist.
            Then we shall ask for bidding for his house:
            Number Four, Breestraat – large, four windows
                  wide,
            With neoclassic pediment; five floors
            Including attic rooms and semi-basement.
            Thirdly, we shall sell his 'paper-art' –
            A feast of prints and drawings by the best
            Italian, Netherlandish, French and German
            Masters, and some hundred sketches by

Rembrandt himself. Shall we begin? Who wants
This statue of a child – I think it's pissing –
By Michelangelo? What am I bid? *(Takes bid)*
(Lights down, then up again slowly, to denote
passing of time)
Nine serving dishes, white; two earthenware
Plates? *(Takes bid)* Six handkerchiefs, three
    tablecloths,
Twelve napkins? *(Takes bid)* Some loose collars,
    three male shirts?
(Takes bid) Two terrestrial globes? *(Takes bid)*
    The death-mask of
Our late Stadholder? *(Takes bid)* A Latin book
By Adrianus Smout, defaced, satiric
Sketches in the margin ...
(Lights down and up again as before)

REMBRANDT   What have you taken so far, Thomas Haringh?

HARINGH   Just over three thousand guilders for your
                    goods.

REMBRANDT   And the house?

HARINGH   Eleven thousand, two eighteen
                 Guilders.

REMBRANDT   Why! That's two thousand guilders
                 less
                 Than I paid for it twenty years ago!

HARINGH   The war, economic depression and these civil
                 Disturbances depress the market. You
                 Have not done badly. What have you been
                    sketching?
                 (Show slide no. 69, of Rembrandt: 'The Phoenix, or
                 The Statue Overthrown' (1658) etching, Schwartz,
                 'Rembrandt's Etchings' (1977) Bartsch 110)
                 A statue thrown down as a phoenix rises
                 From its own funeral pyre. Two angels blow

Their trumpets to announce the miracle.
So you must rise, and bear humiliation
Bravely.

REMBRANDT   What is the new catastrophe?

HARINGH   Your Guild of St. Luke does not like the sale
Of paper art flooding the market. All
Was forced to go as a job lot.

REMBRANDT   How much?

HARINGH   Six hundred guilders was all that it fetched.

REMBRANDT   Aaaah! Less than I'd charge for just one
portrait!
The finest sale of drawings Amsterdam
Has ever seen – or will see – all for just
Six hundred guilders?

HARINGH   Rembrandt, yes. I had
No choice but to obey your Artists' Guild.

REMBRANDT   I am still hopelessly in debt. All gone!
*(Show slide no. 70, of Rembrandt: 'Moses with the
Tablets of the Law' (1659) Bredius 527. Berlin-
Dahlem, Gemäldegalerie)*
Bring down the curtain on the angry law
And smash the system that drives mild men
mad,
Bankrupts creators, closes homes of joy,
And condemns pregnant mothers to abuse,
Wars with our neighbours, forces riots through
Leafy canals and streets of Amsterdam.
Why are we plagued, who only celebrate
Delight in life while daylight fills our skulls,
Too brief a time at best – a flare in the dark.
Why do strong men in power always condemn?
We are not evil; nor are we much good –
And yet we try not to lie to survive.

TITUS   Father, please let me help you. It is time
             To leave. Your face is damp. I'll clean the
                  grime.
             (TITUS *daubs* REMBRANDT*'s tears. Show slide no. 71,
             of Rembrandt: 'The Evangelist Matthew inspired by
             the Angel' (1661) Paris, Musée du Louvre. Exeunt*)

                        SCENE FOURTEEN

             HENDRICKJE *and* CORNELIA.
             Music : Peal of church bells.

CORNELIA   Mother, don't look so sad on Easter Day!

HENDRICKJE   The peal of bells has echoed, and the tower's
             Afternoon shadow startles the clock-face.
             Cornelia, I have seen the notary,
             And in my will you are my heir. I've said
             If you should die without a baby, all
             Goes on to Titus. This way Rembrandt is
             Protected from his creditors.

CORNELIA   No man
             Could have been understood, or cared for,
                  better
             Than father.

HENDRICKJE   Darling daughter, if I fade,
             Will you help him? You know his needs, his
                  failings,
             His concentration inexhaustible.

CORNELIA   You must rest, Mother. Let spring leaves inspire
             You back to blossoming.

HENDRICKJE   I'll try, my love.
             Your father's mighty canvas, quite the most vast
             He's painted, to hang in the gallery
             Of the town hall, has been returned, rejected.

They will not even pay him.

CORNELIA   Why won't they?
It's mad dishonesty to force a man
Create for months on a commissioned theme
And then discard it as an oily rag
Sixteen foot square!

HENDRICKJE   The one-eyed thug he painted did not win
Approval as their hero Claudius Civilis,
Who rose against the Romans long ago.
*(Show slide no. 72, of Rembrandt: 'The Conspiracy
of Claudius Civilis' (c. 1661 – 2) Bredius 482.
Stockholm, Nationalmuseum)*

CORNELIA   But Tacitus tells us he lost an eye!

HENDRICKJE   My breath feels like a mole's whose hill is
        stamped on.
Lazy exhaustion dances on my lungs
Like clogs heaved by obese, drunk aldermen.
Your father's shown that weight upon my chest
In this sad, tender portrait of me.
*(Show slide no. 73, of Rembrandt: 'Hendrickje'
(1660) Bredius 118. New York, Metropolitan
Museum of Art)*

CORNELIA   Mother,
The large air and great sea, this waking earth
And Easter joy will win you back to health!

HENDRICKJE   Prayer, and care, bind us. All we have! Enough.

Fade.

SCENE FIFTEEN

VONDEL, HUYGENS, *and* LIEVENS. *To them* VERMEER.

One lamp on table, centre, casting shadows; faces lit.

VONDEL   Vermeer had hoped to join us, but the riots
            Hurricaning the streets swallow up safety
            To vomit violence since the French attacked
            And burned back half our country to Utrecht.
            We've breached the dykes to flood those
                    polders, and
            Halted French troops a while. Johan de Witt,
            Our modern Oldenbarnevelt, 's been stabbed
            By four youths in The Hague; but he recovers.
            He will need skilled, lychee diplomacy
            To soften words in Louis the XIVth's mouth –
            Republican kissing a monarch's mercy.
            We'll close this door against the might of
                    France
            And share news of who's lost, in blackout vigil,
            Mind-dancing a sonata of the dead.

LIEVENS   Canal-damp sponged Hendrickje's lungs until
            The coming primrose and the violet
            Failed to entice her rally. Hot July
            Stifled her ice-cold. Rembrandt washed her
                    corpse
            That living warmed him through his
                    bankruptcy.

VONDEL   Her life was thirty-seven years of love,
            Selfless, skilled, generous. I am navigating
            My own child back from bankruptcy, and pay
            Some forty thousand guilders to prevent
            Insolvency dissolving honour of
            My only son: but this has left me ruined.

LIEVENS   Van Dyck painted my portrait while I stayed

In England for three years. Then I sailed on
To Antwerp; and chose to come back to you,
My friends in Amsterdam, when my wife died
Leaving me with a tiny son, and bailiffs
Banging the door to seize my home and goods.
I know how bankruptcy corrodes the
    conscience.
Rembrandt sold Saskia's grave in the Oude
    Kirk;
Yet some months later had to rent another
In Westerkirk for devoted Hendrickje.

HUYGENS   Maria Tesselschade, my delight,
Flirtation, sparring love – Eusebia
You named her – has left heart-stopped
    vacancy
In me. May no one ever be so reckless
To measure her immeasurable worth
In words: her brightness would eclipse the sun.
What happened to that nursemaid Rembrandt
    slummed
With for some years before his Hendrickje?

LIEVENS   Geertge Dircx had been a barmaid at
An inn at Hoorn. It's there she met her
    husband –
Long dead. Hendrickje kicked her out of bed
So she could lie by Rembrandt. Geertge sued
Rembrandt for breach of wedding-promise,
    pawned
Some of the jewels, silver, gold that should
Have been bequeathed to Titus on her death.
Why, she was nearly forty! Needed coin!
Two hundred guilders yearly was all she
Received from empty Rembrandt. He
    approached
Her family. They sent a cousin to
Find out from neighbours how she spent her
    nights.
The burgomasters, shocked, agreed that for

Cash maintenance they would confine her in
Gouda's Correction House. It's large. Spare cells
Are hired out to detention on request
Of family. Geertge remained locked up
Five years. Then Rembrandt failed to pay. She
        left,
And died next year.

HUYGENS   Rembrandt is a strange
        man.
He sent me 'Samson Being Blinded' as
A gift: I'd said he was a better painter
Of histories than portraits. Now I'm not
So sure. I sent it back; and half-regret
Poems that I wrote mocking him. The man
Makes little effort to endear himself ...

VERMEER *enters, distressed.*

VERMEER   Thank God I'm with you. Outside, blood leaks to
Canals. A gaoler's maid was sent to Johan
De Witt to say his brother had been tortured
And found 'Not Guilty'. As he could not walk
Now, would his brother please collect him.
Johan de Witt, recovering himself
From stab wounds, brought his coach. Once in
        the prison
Both brothers were seized by the waiting mob,
Beaten, dragged out, piked, used for musket
        practice.
They hanged the naked corpses by the heels,
(Show slide no. 74, of Jan de Baen: 'The Mutilated
Corpses of the De Witt Brothers', (1672) Amsterdam,
Rijksmuseum)
Ripped out their genitals, and ate their fingers.
The streets are quieter now in guilty shock,
Which makes it possible for me to come
To tell you Titus, Rembrandt's son, has died.

HUYGENS   Vermeer, you're brave. Welcome! Thank you.

          Horror
Compounds like yellow, frothy yeast. Titus!
For all his sins, Rembrandt does not deserve
This hideous thunderbolt. Trigland and Smout,
Expelled from Amsterdam, must answer for
Mob violence they stirred up, which has raged
For years now.

VERMEER   Lievens, you should also know
The warehouse storing gunpowder in Delft
Exploded, leaving quarter of the city
Rubble – in the poor part of the town,
Close to my teacher's studio. It took
Into the angry air Carel Fabritius.

VONDEL   More violent death? Fabritius? You are
           Catholic.
We know the tears of Christ spring from his
           wounds
Stabbed by ourselves before we hang him high.
Go, if you will, to Rembrandt. Take good news.
Say we have gifts. Thank him for painting me.
His pilgrimage of suffering comes home
In a great canvas, drying on his easel,
Lit by compassion for my wastrel son.
*(Show slide no. 75, of Rembrandt: 'The Return of the
Prodigal Son' (c. 1669) Bredius 598. St. Petersburg,
Hermitage)*
Youth's full breasts of our speelhouse yield to
           milk
Of prodigal forgiveness as we age
And shared griefs bind us closer. One shoe off,
My son kneels at my feet, wretched, distraught.
My left hand presses him to me; my right
Caresses, beyond words. Isiciata
Leans on her forearm to see if he's ill.
Sappho, thrilled, by the arch looks fondly
           down
Her right hand in its old, excited pose
Self-clutching, unselfconscious. The two men,

Well-dressed and watching, are who would have
        been
Frederik Hendrik and William his son
Had death not blacked their summers'
        afternoon.
It's Rembrandt's generous farewell to all
Our carefree days, rich with the wisdom learned
As we come home to God. Jan Vermeer, go
To see it while you can. Tell Rembrandt we
Bring back to him all that we bought at auction.
Art transcends grief.

VERMEER   He has lost everything
Except one fourteen-year-old daughter who
Cares for him, his and Hendrickje's Cornelia.
A poor man in a rag, all glory gone
Purified into simplicity,
Rembrandt refines his art to ultimate
Perception. He has nothing more to learn.

Fade.

SCENE SIXTEEN

REMBRANDT *painting at easel,* CORNELIA *watching.*
Show slide no. 76, of Rembrandt: 'Self-portrait'
(1669) Bredius 55. London, National Gallery.

CORNELIA   You brisk your brush before you start to paint,
                Nowadays, with a mutter from the Psalms.

REMBRANDT   'O spare me a little, that I may recover my
                        strength:
                Before I go hence, and be no more seen.'

CORNELIA   *(Taking up prayer-book and reading)*
                'Nevertheless, I am alway by thee: for thou
                Hast holden me by my right hand.'

REMBRANDT   That's true,
Cornelia. The turban is too full, too high.
Those lead-white strokes that hang down to the
     right
Must go.

CORNELIA   But are they dry yet?

REMBRANDT   Yes. Two layers
(Painting them) Of brown will not disrupt; only
     conceal.
And that brush in my fingers...

CORNELIA   Father! Don't!
You've swallowed it in darkness – and the hands,
Delicate, parted before, now clumpily clasp!

REMBRANDT   To force the eye up, without that distraction,
On to the face, alone.

CORNELIA   Your stoic eyes,
Like snails as a thrush beak-breaks them on
     stone,
Show pain.

REMBRANDT   You see why Simeon is blind
(Show slide no. 77, of Rembrandt: 'Simeon with the
Christ Child in the Temple (1661 –) Bredius 600.
Stockholm, Nationalmuseum)
On that unfinished canvas, too long left.

CORNELIA   He drinks the light he holds. Finish them both,
Warm in November's reddish-brown of age.
(Fade this final slide of play)
Will you *(Indicating easel)* remould those hands?

REMBRANDT   The light has gone.
This is the end of all I was. Now your
Long task of caring for me is complete,
Closes, like the last touch upon my eyes.
It has been hard for you, I know: and yet

You never frowned or failed me. All was made
Possible, bearable, by one colour – love.
Your patience shows it. I have loved you as
Only a nurturing father nurtured can
As roles exchange. Now is our time to part,
For me to die, for you to live without me.
Dark, cold nights these lost arms once cradled
      you:
Cradle me in your memory today.

REMBRANDT *slowly goes offstage. Wind. Fade to near-dark. Sound of wind increases. Wind dies.* VERMEER *has entered. Raise lights to normal.*

VERMEER   How did he die?

CORNELIA   He went to say a prayer
Beside the mattress, but wind blew the casement
Open. Heavy curtains round the bed
Billowed across the cedar linen-press
And lifted the large mirror, that had held
Geertge's, Saskia's, mother's faces, and
My father's daily, into a thousand fragments.
The storm came for his spirit. He was gone
Where lost flames of all candles dance. No pain.
His passing was more wonderful, and strange,
Than we can understand.

VERMEER   You saw it all.
There is not anyone alive who will
Not mourn. For us that time is now.

CORNELIA   My tears
Are joy he loved me and could say 'Good-bye'.
Perhaps now I may be, dear friend, alone.

Exit VERMEER. *Fade to black as wind builds to smash of mirror off-stage.*

FINIS

Moving Pictures

Review by Nicholas Lambert

OXFORD MAGAZINE, June 1999

This new play by Francis Warner premiered at St John's College in May. It followed the life of Rembrandt van Rijn from his arrival in Amsterdam in 1625 until his death some fifty years later. By tracing his friendships with the great figures of the day, the play explored the interactions of art and life in the Dutch Republic during a period of political turmoil and religious intolerance. Central to this cultural milieu was the Speelhouse, essentially a highly refined brothel, whose patrons included Prince Frederik Hendrik, the poet Joost van den Vondel, the royal advisor Constantijn Huygens, and of course Rembrandt. With such clients the Speelhouse was almost a salon, and this was reflected in the sophistication of the procuress, Isiciata (Laura Knightly-Brown), and her courtesans Sappho and Lesbia (Charlotte Hunt-Grubbe and Sarah McKendrick), whose superbly realised love-song was charged with the most intense eroticism.

Such liberated mores conflicted directly with the prevalent Dutch Calvinism, whose moral severities were personified by the Reverends Smout and Trigland, a ludicrous duo of preachers who combined prurient displeasure with lascivious monologues on mushrooms and the *Song of Songs*. Darren Ormandy and Ian Drysdale played the parts with evident relish which was wonderfully conveyed to the audience. Posing in puritan black, they brought about the suppression of the Speelhouse, thus causing the dissolution of Rembrandt's circle and initiating his decline.

The language bore a certain resemblance to Shakespeare, but was no mere pastiche. While stylised, it came to sound entirely natural thanks to the skill of the actors, at times achieving a lyrical beauty, and its cadences gave a suitable distance to seventeenth-century Holland.

Rembrandt (Simon Kane) had a commanding stage presence, and his defences of art were some of the most convincing I have heard from a fictionalised artist. Van den Vondel (Daniel Cassiel) made a good foil, being so concerned with classical grandeur that he seemed oblivious to the intrinsic value of Rembrandt's work. Crucially, he did not grasp that Rembrandt's depictions owed more to direct observation that to idealised theories of proportion and geometry. The poet's preference for the latter moved Rembrandt to an impassioned justification of his work and his attempt to paint what he saw:

> Truth, in what I see,
> Can be found in a slaughtered ox.

The most striking feature of the staging was the use of Rembrandt's art, in the form of slides, as an integral part of the performance. At a basic level, this established the chronology of the play and showed Rembrandt's artistic development; and in many key scenes it also made explicit the relation between characters on stage and their counterparts in particular paintings. The slides provided a focal point for the audience while at the same time the actors looked outwards, as if the spectator was seeing the scene from a vantage point behind the picture and yet seeing the picture as well. Paintings by Rembrandt's contemporaries were also shown, as were sketches and engravings.

The sketches are crucial to understanding the artist, yet a dramatist who merely wanted illustrations might not have realised this. In *Rembrandt's Mirror*, however, I believe that Warner intended to give further insight beyond Rembrandt's finished pieces: to show the artist at work and the source of his inspiration – the surroundings and people he knew, which were a way of grounding his work in reality and constant subjects for his sketch-book:

> Leave me to find, among the whores and poor,
> Integrity to keep my paintings pure.

Beyond the visual content of the play, its emotional involvement was very strong and there were moments when the audience's identification with the characters became almost palpable. This was exemplified by the shocked silence that greeted the deaths of Rembrandt's first wife and child. Death was an overarching theme of this play, and its impact on Rembrandt's work became pronounced towards the end, especially in his final self-portrait where the experience of the years was etched into his face.

Though the setting was historical and the script evoked the style of Elizabethan verse, this play dealt with issues of much wider relevance. With puritans of all persuasions trying to dictate what artists can depict or say, this play was a timely reminder of the consequences when they gain the upper hand.

This thought-provoking drama renewed my interest in the stage; and by resurrecting a painter in the theatrical afterlife, it provided a singularly convincing defence of art and the artist.

Rembrandt's Mirror

Review by Eva Spain

THEATRE REVIEW, 13.v.1999
(*published by DAILY INFORMATION, OXFORD*)

Rembrandt claimed to paint what he saw, not 'what could be'. With the development of Rembrandt's work as the outline, the play shades in the rich emotional, political and religious detail that influenced his painting. But it goes far beyond being a history of his work.

Rembrandt dwelt amongst whores, princes, preachers and artists, and his life as portrayed in the play provides a ringing defence of a full appreciation of radiance in reality, not in ideals. His visits to whores at 'the poor man's university' are a means 'to keep [his] paintings pure'. The women of pleasure lead a merry, sensuous life, sipping 'bright wine from long blown glasses', until their 'safe, well-ordered' speelhouse is closed by Calvinist preachers, racked by a terrible fear that 'female lust will undermine the state'.

The presence of preachers conveys the religious tensions of the time, but they are also ludicrous figures with their thunderous denunciations of Catholicism and the sexual morals of the populace. Smout, in particular, provides sparks of humour. Amidst bursts of religious fervour, he is moved to make a speech eulogising mushrooms, employing rich sexual imagery to describe them bursting 'shameless and circumcised' from the ground. The preachers contrast with Rembrandt's immersion in common life; in their view 'dignity ignores the rabble'. The naive Vermeer provides a further contrast: he is a bemused figure at his initiation into Rembrandt's world of sensual pleasure at the whorehouse and retains his awkwardness to the end, when he can provide little consolation for Rembrandt's grieving daughter. This lack of emotional and sensual engagement is reflected in his work, which Joost van den Vondel, the poet, compares unfavourably to Rembrandt's as 'tone-deaf to the spirit'.

Rembrandt's paintings are heavily influenced by the vibrant women in his life. The whores are a source of inspiration, as is his first wife Saskia, who in the play proclaims herself 'the patron saint of naughty women'. Saskia dies and is briefly replaced by a mistress, Geertge, and then by a devoted younger mistress, Hendrickje. Meanwhile, the leaders of the state take full advantage of the women at the speelhouse, with William II proclaiming he prefers his women not singly, but 'like pheasants, in a brace'. The princes are also policy-makers and events at the state level and within the speelhouse are finely juxtaposed. In this whorehouse the women 'entice, cook, serve and sew' this being 'woman's image of court policy'.

The tumult in politics and religion ensures that Rembrandt's personal tragedies are mirrored by historical events. By the time the mobs, incited by the Calvinist clergy, take to the streets, Rembrandt has lost his first wife, his son Titus and the devoted Hendrickje, and his property has been auctioned to pay off debts. His friends have their own misfortunes and are thus bound to him in their shared griefs and age. At this stage Rembrandt's work has been 'purified into simplicity'. He now has nothing more to learn.

The play is fabulously detailed and interweaves the joy and tragedy of individuals with the background of political and religious change. The language is rich, with sparks of humour and pertinent observations on love, sensuality, grief, morality and art. This depth is sustained by immaculate and engaging acting and lavish costumes. The shifting scenes afford glimpses of the living reality that Rembrandt sought to crystalise in his work. A few hundred words cannot do this play justice. Go and see it.